MICROSOFT® QUICK C®

□ □ □ □ □

KRIS JAMSA

PUBLISHED BY
Microsoft Press
A Division of Microsoft Corporation
16011 NE 36th Way, Box 97017, Redmond, Washington 98073-9717

Copyright © 1989 by Microsoft Press
All rights reserved. No part of the contents of this book may
be reproduced or transmitted in any form or by any means without
the written permission of the publisher.

Library of Congress Cataloging in Publication Data

Jamsa, Kris A.
Microsoft QuickC.

   1. C (Computer program language)   2. Microsoft QuickC
(Computer program)   I. Title.
QA76.73.C15J356   1989   005.26   89-12134
ISBN 1-55615-200-0

Printed and bound in the United States of America.

1 2 3 4 5 6 7 8 9 WAKWAK 3 2 1 0 9

Distributed to the book trade in the United States by Harper & Row.

Distributed to the book trade in Canada by General Publishing
Company, Ltd.

Distributed to the book trade outside the United States and Canada
by Penguin Books Ltd.

Penguin Books Ltd., Harmondsworth, Middlesex, England
Penguin Books Australia Ltd., Ringwood, Victoria, Australia
Penguin Books N.Z. Ltd., 182-190 Wairau Road, Auckland 10,
New Zealand

British Cataloging in Publication Data available

Microsoft,® Microsoft QuickC,® and MS-DOS® are registered trademarks
of Microsoft Corporation.

Project Editor: Barbara Olsen Browne
Technical Editor: Mary Ottaway

Contents

1: Installing and Starting QuickC
Installing QuickC... 1
Starting QuickC... 3
Using QCL... 3

2: Using QuickC
Command line (accessing).................................. 13
Compiling... 14
Constants (predefined).................................... 19
Debugging 20
Editing keys 24
Environment variables (accessing) 27
Global variables and constants (predefined) 29
Help 32
In-line assembly language................................. 33
Keywords (predefined) 34
Libraries.. 35
Menus.. 36
Operators 40
Pragmas 43
Preprocessor directives 45
printf control sequences................................... 50
Types 51

3: QuickC Libraries and Functions
QuickC include files and the functions they contain 53
QuickC run-time library functions 59

4: QuickC Compiler Error Messages
Fatal error messages...................................... 119
Compilation error messages................................ 125
Warning messages 147

Introduction

This Quick Reference provides you with information about Microsoft QuickC that programmers working with QuickC will use on a daily basis. It's divided into four sections.

Section 1 explains how to install and start QuickC and use the QCL command line compiler. Section 2 covers working in the QuickC environment, including using the QuickC pull-down menus, debugging your programs, and using program development techniques for large programs or for programs that use object file libraries. In addition, Section 2 explains the QuickC compiler, compiler restrictions and pragmas, accessing command line arguments in the QuickC environment, using DOS environment variables, and including in-line assembly language in your programs.

Section 3 provides information about the run-time library functions and summarizes the include files. Section 4 lists and explains the QuickC compiler error messages.

If you use QuickC frequently, you'll want to have this pocket reference by your side.

The following notational conventions apply to the entries in this guide:

Convention	*Meaning*
Italic	Represents variables whose values you supply.
Brackets []	Encloses an optional variable; do not type the brackets.
Brackets <>	Encloses either variables for which you must provide values (do not type the brackets) or the name of a header file (type the brackets).
Braces { }	Encloses multiple variables that are separated by pipes (!); choose only one of the variables, and do not type the braces.

1: *Installing and Starting QuickC*

Installing QuickC

After you install QuickC using SETUP on QuickC's Setup disk, be sure to define the DOS environment variables PATH, LIB, and INCLUDE in your AUTOEXEC.BAT file so that they reference the correct DOS subdirectories. The SETUP program helps by creating a file named NEW-VARS.BAT that specifies the paths that you should add to your AUTOEXEC.BAT file. Also, be sure that the CONFIG.SYS file contains the FILES and BUFFERS configuration commands, with minimum values of 20 and 10, respectively, as shown below:

    FILES=20
    BUFFERS=10

The SETUP program creates a file called NEW-CONF.SYS, which creates the above FILES and BUFFERS lines that should be added to your CONFIG.SYS file. To enhance performance, most users will want to assign a value of 25 to BUFFERS to create 25 work areas in memory in which to store data when reading and writing on disk.

Memory models

The amount of memory that your program needs for code and data differs depending upon the application you are creating. As a result, QuickC supports several different memory models. When you install QuickC, you must specify the models for which you plan to program. The SETUP program builds a combined library (containing library functions that can be called from your programs) for each specified memory model. If you need to use a memory model whose library you did not build when you installed QuickC, you can run SETUP with the /L option to build the necessary library.

Put simply, a program's memory model specifies the number of 64 KB data and code segments that the program can use. QuickC by default uses the small memory model, which allows the program to use one 64 KB data segment and one 64 KB code segment. The small memory model is sufficient for most applications.

The remaining memory models allow multiple data or multiple code segments, or both; therefore, your program code size or data size can be quite large. This capacity, however, is not without costs. Because the programs can access both the code segment and the data segment values, accessing the code or data requires more complex addressing. This addressing overhead makes the programs run more slowly, so program development remains a trade-off between size and speed. The following table lists the QuickC memory models, the number of data and code segments each model can use, and the QCL options that, when used in the QCL command from the command line, specify the memory model:

Model	*Data Segments*	*Code Segments*	*QCL Option*
Small	1	1	/AS
Medium	1	Multiple	/AM
Compact	Multiple	1	/AC
Large	Multiple	Multiple	/AL
Huge*	Multiple	Multiple	/AH

* allows data items larger than 64 KB

Each time QuickC executes a program, it defines one of the following constants, depending upon which memory model the program uses:

Constant	*Memory Model*
M_I86SM	Small
M_I86MM	Medium
M_I86CM	Compact
M_I86LM	Large
M_I86HM	Huge

You can determine in your program which memory model is in use by noting which of the above constants is defined. When the huge model is used, both M_I86LM and M_I86HM are defined.

See also: Constants (predefined), Editing keys, Using QCL

Starting QuickC

Use the following format to start QuickC:

QC [/b] [/nohi] [/h] [/g] [/k:<*editor.key*>] [*sourcefile*]

- The QC /b option directs QuickC to use a black-and-white screen display.

- The QC /nohi option disables high-intensity colors for systems, such as LCD, with monochrome monitors that do not support high-density colors.

- The QC /h option directs QuickC to use as many lines on the display as possible. EGA screens, for example, can support 43 lines as well as the default of 25 lines.

- The QC /g option directs QuickC to refresh its video display at a faster rate. This option is useful if you have a machine that can update more quickly than the standard AT, whose rate is used as the QuickC default. If you use this option and see "snow" on your screen, your hardware cannot handle the speed. Start QuickC again without using this option.

- The QC /k:<*editor.key*> option lets you change the editor that you use in the QuickC environment. The QuickC environment supports keyboard combinations for four editors: the QuickC editor, the Microsoft editor, BRIEF, and Epsilon. To select an editor other than the default QuickC editor when you start QuickC, use the /k option to specify the KEY file for the editor. The four KEY files are QC.KEY, ME.KEY, BRIEF.KEY, and EPSILON.KEY.

- The QC *sourcefile* option specifies the C source file that QuickC will load. If the source file doesn't exist, QuickC asks if you want to create it.

Using QCL

Most QuickC programmers develop their programs in the QuickC environment. After you successfully test the program, you might want to compile and link the program from the command line. You can compile and link using the QCL command, or you can suppress the linking with the /c option and use QCL for compiling only. Then invoke the linker using the LINK command.

The QCL compiler

The format of the QCL command is as follows:

QCL [options] *filename(s)* [/link link options]

QCL supports the following compiler options:

Options

Memory Model Options

Option	Description
/AS	Selects small model—uses one data segment and one code segment
/AM	Selects medium model—uses one data segment and multiple code segments
/AC	Selects compact model—uses multiple data segments and one code segment; data items must be smaller than 64 KB
/AL	Selects large model—uses multiple data segments and multiple code segments; data items must be smaller than 64 KB
/AH	Selects huge model—uses multiple data segments and multiple code segments; data segments can be any size

Optimization Options

Option	Description
/O	Enables optimization—minimizes execution time; may be followed by any combination of the letters "d," "l," "t," and "x," whose effects this table describes below
/Od	Disables optimization—does not reorganize code when compiling; useful for debugging
/Ol	Enables loop optimization—stores frequently used loops in registers
/Ot	Enables optimization—performs shift operations on long operands and minimizes execution time
/Ox	Enables maximum optimization—same as /Otl /Gs

Code Generation Options

Option	Description
/G0	Generates 8086/8088 instructions—enables instruction set for 8086 and 8088 processors; default for QuickC
/G2	Generates 80286 instructions—enables instruction set for 80286 processor

(continued)

Code Generation Options *continued*

Option	*Description*
/Gc	Specifies use of Pascal calling and naming conventions—creates code that pushes function's parameters onto stack from left to right
/Gi	Performs incremental compilation—compiles only changed functions in each source file; this option ignored if you use any optimization option
/Gs	Disables stack checking—removes the code used to check the stack
/Gt[*value*]	Defines data threshold—allocates to new data segment all data items that are larger than or equal to *value*; if *value* omitted, default threshold is 256; if this option not used, threshold is 32,767

Output File Options

Option	*Description*
/Fb[*bound_EXE_filename*]	Binds a FAPI (Family Applications Program Interface) program—creates an executable file whose name is specified by *bound_EXE_filename* and that can run both in OS/2 protected mode and in DOS 3.x (also called real mode)
/Fe<*EXE_filename*>	Assigns name specified by *EXE_filename* to executable file—replaces default name, which is base name of the first filename on the command line plus extension EXE
/Fm[*map_file*]	Creates a linker map file—creates a file named *map_file* that contains a list of segments in order of appearance within load module
/Fo<*OBJ_filename*>	Assigns name specified by *OBJ_filename* to object file—replaces default name, which is base name of source file that corresponds to object file plus extension OBJ

Preprocessor Options

Option	*Description*
/C	Removes no comments—preserves comments throughout preprocessing; valid only when used with the /E, /EP, or /P option

(continued)

Preprocessor Options *continued*

Option   Description

/E   Preprocesses and copies output to stdout; does not compile—performs only preprocessing; preprocessor also surrounds both included files and lines removed by preprocessor directives with the #line preprocessor directive; enables compiler to give correct line numbers when errors are found

/EP   Preprocesses and copies output to stdout; does not compile or include the #line preprocessor directive—performs only preprocessing

/P   Preprocesses and copies output to file—creates file whose base name is same as source file and whose extension is I; performs only preprocessing

/I<*directory*>

    Specifies search directory—searches directory specified by *directory* for include files before searching current directory and directories specified by INCLUDE environment variable

/X   Searches for no include files—searches neither in current directory nor in directories defined by INCLUDE environment variable

/D<*identifier*>[={*string* ¦ *number*}]

    Defines macro or constant—gives macro or constant the name specified by *identifier*; if you omit equal sign and *string* or equal sign and *number*, *identifier* defined with a value of 1; if no string or number follows equal sign, definition of *identifier* removed

/U<*constant_name*>

    Undefines predefined constant specified by *constant_name*

/u   Undefines all predefined constants

Language Options

Option   Description

/Ze   Enables language extensions—allows use of QuickC features that are extensions of ANSI C standard; default

/Za   Disables language extensions—disables QuickC features that extend ANSI C standard; useful when you plan to port program to another system

/Zr   Checks for NULL pointers and out-of-range far pointers—checks all pointers in program except those preceded by check_pointer pragma when parameter to pragma is "off"

(continued)

Language Options *continued*

Option *Description*

/Zd   Includes information for debugging with SYMDEB—gives source code line numbers

/Zi   Includes symbolic debugger information for use with CodeView or QuickC debugger—gives both full symbol-table information and source code line numbers

/Zs   Checks source file syntax only; does not generate code—provides quick way to find syntax errors

/Zp[{1¦2¦4}]
       Packs structures to enhance memory utilization—uses 1-, 2-, or 4-byte boundaries in which to store each structure; default is 2-byte boundary

/Zl   Removes information about default library from object file—saves small amount of space; useful when you build your own library

Floating-Point Options

Option *Description*

/FPi   Replaces mathematic function calls with in-line 8087/80287 coprocessor instructions and places name of emulator library in object file—uses coprocessor at run time if coprocessor is present; otherwise, defaults to emulator

/FPi87 Replaces mathematic function calls with in-line 8087/80287 coprocessor instructions—requires coprocessor at run time

Miscellaneous Options

Option *Description*

/c   Compiles to OBJ file only—does not link object files, so no executable file created

/W<level> Disables warning messages—a *level* of 0 suppresses all warning messages; options /W1, /W2, and /W3 allow, successively, more messages; default is 1

/w   Suppresses all warning messages—same as /W0

/HELP Lists compile options—processes all information on command line and then lists most commonly used options

/Tc <filename>
       Specifies C source file—gives name of a C source file; useful if source filename does not have C extension

(continued)

Miscellaneous Options continued

Option	Description
/J	Changes default *char* type—changes default of QuickC type *char* from *signed* to *unsigned*; identifier _CHAR_UNSIGNED is defined if this option used
/NT <*textname*>	Names text segment—gives name *textname* to code (i.e., text) segment of each object file; in most cases, should be used only with medium, large, and huge memory models

Linker Options

Option	Description
/F<*stack_size*>	Specifies desired stack size in bytes—value of *stack_size* must be hexadecimal number; default is 2 KB
/Li	Performs incremental linking—links only changed files; incremental linking also performed when you use /Gi option for incremental compilation
/Lp	Links to create protected-mode executable file—creates files for use in OS/2 protected-mode environment
/Lr	Links to create compatibility-mode executable—creates files for use in OS/2 real-mode and DOS environments
/link [command line linker options or library names]	Specifies linker options or additional libraries, or both—uses options listed in the "Command Line Linker Options" table included later in this section

Filenames used on the QCL command line

You can specify many files on the QCL command line. What QCL does with a file depends upon that filename's extension. The following table explains these actions:

Extension	Type of File	Action
C	C source file	QCL compiles the file.
OBJ	C object file	QCL passes the file to the linker for linking.
LIB	Stand-alone C library file	QCL passes the file to the linker for linking with object files.
No extension, or an extension other than C, OBJ, or LIB	C object file	QCL passes the file to the linker for linking.

The CL environment variable

Each time you compile a program from the command line, QCL checks the DOS environment to see if you have defined the CL environment variable. If you have defined it, QCL uses the options that are in the entry definition during compilation. To define the CL entry, use the DOS SET command. For example, the following entry directs QCL to enable optimization and to use the medium memory model each time QCL compiles a program:

    C> SET CL=/Ox /AM

The command line linker

Using the DOS LINK command, you can link your files from the command line. This command's format is as follows:

  LINK *obj_filename(s)* [,[*exe_filename*] [,[*map_filename*]
      [,[*lib_filename(s)*]]]][;]

The following table describes the files that the LINK command uses:

File	Extension	Description
obj_filename(s)	OBJ, LIB, or none	One or more files to be linked, separated by plus signs or spaces. If a library file is included in this section, every object in the library module is linked to the other specified object files.
exe_filename	EXE	Name of the executable file. The default name is the base name of the first object file plus the extension EXE.
map_filename	MAP	Name of the map file. The file contains a list of segments in the order in which they appear in the object file.
lib_filename(s)	LIB	One or more stand-alone libraries, separated by plus signs or spaces. These libraries will be used to resolve external references in your program.

You can specify default values for fields that remain on the command line by placing a semicolon (;) on the line. The defaults are as follows: an executable file whose base name is that of the first object file, no map file, and the default libraries specified in the object files. Use commas as placeholders for the fields. QuickC uses the default if a comma is in place, except in the *map_filename* field. For the *map_filename* field, QuickC creates a map file whose base name is that of the executable file and whose extension is MAP. For example, to specify a new library but use the default names for the executable and map files, place commas in the executable and map file fields and type the library name.

Just as the QCL command line compiler supports many options, so does the DOS linker. The following options, listed in alphabetic order, are common to QuickC programs:

Command Line Linker Options

Option   Description

/BA[TCH]   Directs the linker to continue processing when it cannot locate a specific file, instead of prompting the user to enter a new path.

/CO[DEVIEW]
           Directs the linker to create an executable file that you can debug using CodeView or the QuickC debugger. You must have used the /Zi option in the QCL command.

/CP[ARMAXALLOC]:<*paragraphs*>
           Defines the number of 16-byte paragraphs that the program requires. The linker usually requests the maximum number of paragraphs available. This option allows you to limit the number.

/DO[SSEG] Directs the linker to order the segments according to the Microsoft languages standard. This option is the default when you link to a QuickC library.

/E[XEPACK]
           Directs the linker to remove sequences of repeated bytes and to optimize the load-time-relocation table.

/F[ARCALLTRANSLATION]
           Directs the linker to optimize far calls to procedures that appear in the same segment as the calling procedure.

/HE[LP]   Directs the linker to display a list of the supported options.

(continued)

Command Line Linker Options *continued*

Option   Description

/INF[ORMATION]
> Directs the linker to display information about the linking process, such as the names of the object files that are being linked.

/LI[NENUMBERS]
> Directs the linker to create a map file that contains line numbers that are associated with each listed symbol. You must have used the /Zd option in the QCL command. Use this option when debugging using SYMDEB.

/M[AP]   Directs the linker to create a map file that contains two lists of the symbols that are defined in the object file. One list is sorted by name, the other by address. If you do not use this option, the map file that QuickC creates contains only a list of segments.

/NOD[EFAULTLIBRARYSEARCH][:*filename*]
> Directs the linker not to search for unresolved references in any library specified in the object file. If a filename is specified, the linker searches all libraries specified in the object file except *filename*.

/NOE[XTDICTIONARY]
> Directs the linker not to search the extended dictionary, which is an internal list of symbol locations maintained by the linker.

/NOF[ARCALLTRANSLATION]
> Ensures that the linker does not optimize far calls to procedures that appear in the same segment as the calling procedure.

/NOI[GNORECASE]
> Directs the linker to distinguish between lowercase and uppercase identifier names.

/NOP[ACKCODE]
> Ensures that the linker does not pack neighboring code segments.

/O[VERLAYINTERRUPT]:<*number*>
> Redefines the interrupt number used for passing controls to overlays. The default is 63. The number must be in the range 0 through 255.

(continued)

Command Line Linker Options *continued*

Option   Description

/PAC[KCODE][:*value*]
: For efficiency, directs the linker to group neighboring code segments. The value specifies a group's maximum size. The default value is 65,530. This option is useful only when you use medium-model or large-model programs.

/PAU[SE]
: Directs the linker to pause before writing the EXE file on a disk so that you can change disks.

/SE[GMENTS]:<*number*>
: Defines the maximum number of segments that the program can use. The default is 128. The value must be in the range 1 through 3072.

/ST[ACK]:<*size*>
: Specifies the size of the stack space in the range 0 through 65,535. The default stack size is 2048.

The linker lets you abbreviate options, but you must include sufficient letters for the linker to distinguish between the options. In the above table, the minimum abbreviation for each option is shown to the left of the option's bracketed portion. Although the linker supports additional options, do not use them if you have compiled with the QuickC compiler.

See also: Compiling, Constants (predefined), Installing QuickC, Pragmas, Preprocessor directives

2: *Using QuickC*

Command line (accessing)

Most programmers perform their initial program development from the QuickC environment rather than from the command line. The Run/Debug command on the Options menu lets you specify the command line that QuickC uses each time you run a program from within the QuickC environment. When you choose the Run/Debug command, QuickC displays a dialog box that prompts you to enter the command line. Type the arguments that you want QuickC to pass to your program. After you specify a command line, that command line remains in effect until you exit the QuickC environment.

C has the ability to access in a program the command line that the user entered to start the program. Each time you run a C program, the program executes a small header routine that separates the command line into distinct arguments. Then it passes two parameters to *main()*. These two parameters are a count of the number of command line arguments and an array of pointers to each command line argument. To access these parameters within your program, declare *main()* as shown below:

```
main(int argc, char *argv[])
```

The *argc* variable contains a count of the number of command line arguments. And the *argv* variable is an array of pointers to each command line argument. Note that if you are using DOS version 3.0 or later, the first argument on any command line is the drive specification and the program's full pathname.

If you use the following command line, the *argc* variable will be given a value of 3:

```
C> MYCOPY SOURCE.DAT TARGET.DAT
```

The elements of the *argv* array will point to the following strings:

argv[0] points to "C:\MYCOPY.EXE"
argv[1] points to "SOURCE.DAT"
argv[2] points to "TARGET.DAT"

The following program, ECHOTEST.C, displays each of the command line arguments:

```c
/* ECHOTEST.C */

main(int argc, char *argv[])
{
    int i;

    for (i = 0; i < argc; i++)
        puts(argv[i]);
}
```

If you run the ECHOTEST program from the DOS prompt and include the arguments A, B, C, and D, the command line and subsequent output appear on your screen as follows:

```
C> ECHOTEST A B C D
C:\ECHOTEST.EXE
A
B
C
D
```

See also: Compiling

Compiling

The following table describes the QuickC commands from which you can choose to compile a program:

Command   Description

Compile File (Make menu)
: Creates object file for current source file; does not link.

Build Program (Make menu)
: Builds (compiles and links) all out-of-date files specified in program list; when program list not available, current file is built if out of date.

Rebuild All (Make menu)
: Builds (compiles and links) all files specified in program list; when program list not available, current file is built.

Go (Run menu)
: Starts or continues program execution; if program has changed, gives user option of rebuilding.

(continued)

Command   Description

Restart (Run menu)
: Builds (compiles and links) any file specified in program list (or current file, when program list not available) if file has not been built before or is out of date. If file has been built before, sets the point at which execution will begin to first line of program.

Compiler and linker options

The following two tables describe the compiler and linker flags that you can set in the QuickC Compiler Flags and Linker Flags dialog boxes. To use these dialog boxes, choose the Make command from the Options menu and then choose the name of the dialog box that you want to open.

Compiler Flags

Flag   Description

Memory Model
: Choose the memory model (small, medium, compact, large, or huge) to be used. Small is the default.

Warn Level
: Choose the level of warning message to be used during compilation. Levels give progressively more messages. For example, choosing Level 0 turns off all warnings, and choosing Level 3 displays all possible warnings.

C language
: Choose ANSI Compatibility to direct the compiler to give warnings for all code that is not part of the ANSI standard for C. Choose MS Extensions to allow Microsoft's extensions to the C language.

Debug Info
: Choose CodeView Info to prepare the object file for debugging with the CodeView or QuickC debugger. Choose Line Numbers Only to prepare the object file for debugging with SYMDEB.

Pointer Check
: Choose this flag to enable checking for null or out-of-range pointers.

Incremental Compile
: Choose this flag to compile only files that have been changed.

Optimizations
: Choose On to optimize the execution speed. Choose Full to optimize more completely by storing in registers the loops that you use frequently. Choose Off to turn off optimization.

(continued)

Compiler Flags *continued*

Flag — *Description*

Stack Check — Choose this flag to call a stack-checking routine that verifies whether enough stack space is available each time the program enters a function.

Defines — Type the definition of a macro or constant.

Linker Flags

Flag — *Description*

Ignore Case — Choose this flag to turn off case sensitivity.

Pause — Choose this flag when you want the linker to pause and give you time to insert a new floppy disk before the linker writes the executable file.

Extended Dictionary — Choose this flag to enable the linker to search its internal dictionary for symbol definitions. If you are creating your own library, be sure this option is disabled.

Stack Size — Type the stack size. The default is 2 KB.

CodeView Info — Choose this flag to prepare the executable file for debugging with the CodeView or QuickC debugger.

Map File — Choose this flag to create a map file that contains a listing of the program's symbols.

Incremental Link — Choose this flag to link only files that have been changed.

Syntax errors

If your source file contains syntax errors, QuickC aborts compiling and highlights the program lines that contain errors. You can move from one error location to another using either the Next Error and Previous Error commands from the Search menu or the Shift+F3 (Next Error) and Shift+F4 (Previous Error) keyboard combinations. After you correct all the syntax errors, recompile your program.

Compiling multiple source files with a program list

As you develop programs, you can place functions in their own source files to improve your file organization and to allow several different programs to access the same functions. One way to link several files is to use the #include preprocessor directive.

Although #include does allow you to separate source files, it has a disadvantage: The compiler must recompile all the source code each time you compile the program, often taking up valuable development time. As an alternative, you can use a program list to link several files and create one executable program. Using the program list, QuickC can decide which files need to be recompiled. For example, if a source file in the list has not changed since it was compiled to create an object file, QuickC does not recompile that source file.

A program list contains the names of the files used to create the executable program. This list can contain C source files, object files, or library files. QuickC stores the information that's in a program list in a file that has the extension MAK. Both the QuickC NMAKE programming utility and QuickC can use this file.

To create a program list, choose the Set Program List command from the Make menu and, in the File Name box, type the base name of the .MAK file that you want to create. Press Enter. If the file already exists, QuickC loads the program list and makes it the current list. If the file does not exist, QuickC asks if you want to create the .MAK file. If you choose Yes, QuickC opens the Edit Program List dialog box so that you can specify the files to include in the list. You specify a file by typing its filename in the File Name box and choosing the Add/Delete option (or pressing Enter if the option is highlighted). You can also highlight a filename in the File List box and choose the Add/Delete option (or press Enter if the option is highlighted). To delete a file from the program list, highlight the filename in the Program List box and choose the Add/Delete option (or press Enter if the option is highlighted). When your program list is complete, choose the Save List option and press Enter to save your program list in a .MAK file.

After you create the program list, choose the Build Program command from the Make menu to compile and link your program. Then choose the Go command (F5) from the Run menu to execute the program.

Let's look at an example of creating multiple source files and a program list. First create a file called DISPLAY.C that contains the following:

```
/* display.c */

void display(int a)
{
    printf("%d\n", a);
}
```

Save the file, and create a new file called TESTLIST.C that contains the following:

```
/* testlist.c */
main()
{
    int i;

    for (i = 0; i < 10; i++)
        display(i);
}
```

Save the file. Next choose the Set Program List command from the Make menu. Type *TESTLIST* in the File Name box to create a file called TESTLIST.MAK. After you choose Yes to create the .MAK file, QuickC opens the Edit Program List dialog box. In File Name, type *TESTLIST.C* and press Enter. Next type *DISPLAY.C* and press Enter. Choose the Save List option, and press Enter. Choose the Build Program command from the Make menu to compile and link the specified files in the program list. When QuickC finishes the build operation, you can press F5 (Go) to execute the program.

Using the QuickC editor, change the conditional expression of the loop in the program from 10 to 100, as shown below:

```
for (i = 0; i < 100; ++i)
    display(i);
```

Save the file, and choose the Build Program command again from the Make menu. Because TESTLIST.C is the only file that has changed, it's the only file that QuickC must recompile. QuickC uses the previous DISPLAY.OBJ file during linking because DISPLAY.C has not changed. Using a program list also allows you to access library files from the QuickC environment.

Compiler Restrictions

The QuickC compiler places only a few restrictions on your programs, as the following table summarizes:

Program Item *Description*
Identifiers   An identifier is a name. QuickC restricts the length of a C identifier name to 31 characters. If an identifier name exceeds 31 characters, QuickC displays a warning message and truncates the name.

(continued)

Program Item   Description

Structure declarations
: C structures can contain references to other structure types; this arrangement is called a nested structure declaration. QuickC restricts the level of nested structure declarations to 10.

Macro size
: QuickC restricts a macro's length to a maximum of 1024 bytes.

QCL /D
: QuickC restricts to 20 the number of macros that you can define using the /D compiler option.

Macro parameters
: QuickC restricts the number of macro parameters to 31.

Preprocessor argument length
: QuickC restricts the length of a preprocessor argument to 256 bytes.

Preprocessor directives
: QuickC restricts the level of the nested #if, #ifdef, and #ifndef preprocessor directives to 32.

Include files
: The #include preprocessor directive specifies a source file that the preprocessor should include. This source file can contain additional #include directives, the occurrence of which is called a nested include. QuickC restricts the level of nested include files to 10.

Include file search path
: The INCLUDE environment entry in your AUTOEXEC.BAT file indicates which subdirectories QuickC will search for include files. QuickC restricts the number of paths in the INCLUDE entry to 20.

See also: Constants (predefined), Libraries, Pragmas, Preprocessor directives, Using QCL

Constants (predefined)

QuickC lets you define your own constants via the #define preprocessor directive. QuickC also predefines additional constants whose values you can use in your programs, as the following table shows:

Constant	Meaning
_QC	Defined if using QuickC compiler
MSDOS	Defined if using MS-DOS operating system
M_I8086	Defined if target machine is an 8086; see the /G0 compiler switch
M_I286	Defined if target machine is an 80286; see the /G2 compiler switch
M_I86	Defined if target machine is a member of Intel family
M_I86SM	Defined if using small memory model
M_I86MM	Defined if using medium memory model
M_I86CM	Defined if using compact memory model
M_I86LM	Defined if using large memory model
M_I86HM	Defined if using huge memory model
NO_EXT_KEYS	Defined if Microsoft extended keywords are disabled; see the /Za compiler switch
_CHAR_UNSIGNED	Defined when the default char type is unsigned; see the /J compiler switch

The constants shown in the table above are defined only if a specific condition exists. You can test to see whether the constants are defined by using the #ifdef and #ifndef preprocessor directives. QuickC also supports a set of constants, called global variables, that are always defined.

See also: Global variables and constants (predefined), Using QCL

Debugging

One of QuickC's most convenient features is its built-in debugging capability. Using one or two QuickC menu commands, you can eliminate the need for lines of debug *printf* statements in your programs. Commands for debugging are provided on the Run and Debug menus.

The following is a list of the commands that you can use to debug your programs:

- Continue to Cursor (Run menu or F7)—Executes the program to the line that has the cursor.

- Trace Into (Run menu or F8)—Executes the program line by line, stepping through all functions.

- Step Over (Run menu or F10)—Executes the program line by line, stepping over functions to the next line in the program.

- Calls (Debug menu)—Lists the calls in your program that lead up to the current statement. This command can be used only when execution stops at a statement during a debugging session.

- Breakpoint (Debug menu or F9)—Sets a point in your program at which execution halts. To set a breakpoint, either press F9 on the line at which you want execution to stop or choose the Breakpoint command to open a dialog box that prompts you for the breakpoint's line number.

- Watchpoint (Debug menu)—Sets an expression that, when evaluated to true, halts execution.

- Watch Value (Debug menu)—Places a variable (or any C expression) and its value in the Watch window. QuickC updates the value as you step through the program.

- Modify Value (Debug menu)—Changes the value of a variable or expression.

- History On (Debug menu)—Creates a record of the debugging session, starting at the execution of the program. QuickC records both debugger commands and all typed input. (To record only one or the other, choose the Run/Debug command from the Options menu and set the Debug History options.) Use Shift+F8 to display the previous history point and Shift+F10 to move to the next history point.

- Undo (Debug menu)—Erases the last debugger command from the history when QuickC is recording the history.

- Replay (Debug menu)—Replays all or part of a debug session when QuickC is recording the history, starting the replay at the execution of the program. If you used Shift+F8 and Shift+F10 to move through the history, the replay halts where you stopped browsing.

- Truncate User Input (Debug menu)—Clears all or part of the input that was recorded in QuickC's history. To clear all, choose the Restart command from the Run menu and then choose the Truncate User Input command. To clear only from a specific point, use

Shift+F8 and Shift+F10 to move through the history to the point at which you want to begin clearing the input. Next choose the Replay command from the Debug menu, and then choose Truncate User Input.

So that you have a C program to use in the following example debugging session, create a file called SUM.C that contains the following:

```c
/* SUM.C */

main()
{
    int count;
    int sum = 0;

    for (count = 0; count < 10; count++)
        sum += count;

    printf("%d %d\n", sum, count);
}
```

Although this program is not complex, its contents allow you to experiment with several key debugging concepts. First, note that *count* and *sum* are the two variables used most often in this example. As a result, you might want to keep track of these variable's values. Using the QuickC debugger, you can select each of these variables as a watch value. QuickC displays each variable's name and value in the Watch window after each statement as you execute the program one statement at a time. Using watch values provides the same result as inserting *printf* statements that print the value of each variable after every statement in your program. To specify a watch value, choose the Watch Value command from the Debug menu. QuickC then displays a dialog box that prompts you to enter an expression. For this example, type the variable name *sum* in the Expression text box and then press Enter. Repeat the process by choosing the Watch Value command and typing the expression for the variable *count*; QuickC now tracks the values of these two variables.

To step through the program's statements one at a time and see how the watch values are modified, choose the Trace Into command from the Run menu. QuickC executes your program, pausing at each line of source code. To continue to the next line, press F8. As you trace the first few lines of code, note how your watch variables' values change. Using watch variables and tracing your entire program's code will help you resolve errors in your programs.

As your program executes, conditions might arise about which you want QuickC to notify you immediately. Such conditions are called watchpoints. To specify a watchpoint, choose the Watchpoint command from the Debug menu. QuickC then displays a dialog box that prompts you to enter an expression. For this example, type the following in the Expression text box and then press Enter:

```
count > 5
```

QuickC informs you that the expression is illegal. It's illegal because it contains a local variable that is not defined until the program executes. You can safely ignore the warning. When the *count* variable exceeds 5, QuickC displays a dialog box that tells you so. Using the Trace Into command (F8) from the Run menu again, step through the program one statement at a time. When QuickC displays the dialog box informing you that your watchpoint has occurred, choose the OK button to continue.

To remove a watchpoint, choose the Watchpoint command from the Debug menu. Move the cursor next to the "count > 5" expression, and press the spacebar to highlight the expression. Next, choose the Add/Delete option and press Enter to remove your watch point.

Often it's not practical to trace an entire program. You would not want to step through every line in your code, for example, if you knew that you would find the error near the end of the program. To mark a location in your program at which QuickC will stop the execution, you can use the Breakpoint command from the Debug menu. After QuickC encounters the breakpoint in your program, you can trace through the statements of the program from that location.

To set a breakpoint, position the cursor on the line that you want to mark. Next, choose the Breakpoint command (F9) from the Debug menu. QuickC highlights the line to indicate the breakpoint. For this example, set the breakpoint at the *printf* statement and then choose the Go command (F5) from the Run menu to execute the program. QuickC performs each of the statements that precede the breakpoint and halts execution at the breakpoint. (In the example, execution stops at the *printf* statement.) To resume execution, choose the Go command (F5) again or choose the Trace Into command (F8) to begin tracing through the rest of the program.

To remove a breakpoint, position the cursor on the line that contains the breakpoint and choose the Breakpoint command from the Debug menu. QuickC removes the breakpoint and the line's highlight.

This section includes an in-depth discussion of only a few of QuickC's debugging commands. With this foundation, however, you should be able to use the debugger to isolate many of your program errors.

Editing keys

Creating a set of keyboard combinations

QuickC allows you to modify any of the four .KEY files that define the keyboard combinations for editor functions. The four files are QC.KEY, ME.KEY, BRIEF.KEY, and EPSILON.KEY, which are associated respectively with the QuickC editor, the Microsoft editor, BRIEF, and Epsilon. To create keyboard combinations that you can use in QuickC, use the MKKEY command from the DOS prompt. When you use MKKEY, you must include the following three options:

Option　*Description*

-c　　Specifies one of the two types of conversion that QuickC can perform—either binary to ASCII (ba) or ASCII to binary (ab)

-i　　Specifies the input file to the MKKEY command—either a text file or a .KEY binary file

-o　　Specifies the output file from the MKKEY command—either a text file or a .KEY binary file

To convert the QC.KEY file from binary to ASCII so that you can edit it, use the following MKKEY command:

```
C> MKKEY -c ba -i QC.KEY -o MYKEYS.TXT
```

Using any editor, you can edit the MYKEYS.TXT file to define keyboard combinations. After you define the combinations, use the MKKEY command again to create a file that has the KEY extension and that contains your keyboard combination definitions:

```
C> MKKEY -c ab -i MYKEYS.TXT -o MYKEYS.KEY
```

After you create this file, you can specify it when you start QuickC and then use the keyboard combinations (that you defined in the MYKEYS file) when you work in QuickC:

```
C> QC /k:MYKEYS.KEY
```

QuickC editor keyboard combinations

When you use the QuickC editor, QuickC supports the following keyboard combinations:

Editing

Function	*Keyboard Combination*
Undo editing commands performed on current line.	Ctrl+QL
Toggle insert mode.	Ctrl+V or Ins
Change selected text.	Ctrl+QA
Locate next occurrence of a word.	Ctrl+L
Move a highlighted block of characters one tab setting.	Tab
Insert any character, including one such as Ctrl+C.	Ctrl+P followed by Ctrl+character
Break current line into two lines that have matching indentation, moving cursor to beginning of second line.	Ctrl+M
Break current line into two lines that have matching indentation, leaving cursor at end of first line.	Ctrl+N
Backspace and delete character to left of cursor's position.	Ctrl+H or Backspace
Delete the character at cursor's position.	Ctrl+G or Delete
Delete one word.	Ctrl+T
Erase to end of line.	Ctrl+QY
Erase current line.	Ctrl+Y
Cancel prefix tables to abort choosing function whose keyboard combination begins with Ctrl+K or Ctrl+U.	Ctrl+KU or Ctrl+QU
Set first bookmark.	Ctrl+K0
Set second bookmark.	Ctrl+K1
Set third bookmark.	Ctrl+K2
Set fourth bookmark.	Ctrl+K3

Scrolling

Function	*Keyboard Combination*
Scroll text down.	Ctrl+Z or Ctrl+down arrow key
Scroll text up.	Ctrl+W or Ctrl+up arrow key
Move cursor right one character.	Ctrl+D or right arrow key
Move cursor left one character.	Ctrl+S or left arrow key

(continued)

Scrolling *continued*
Function / *Keyboard Combination*

Function	Keyboard Combination
Move cursor right one word.	Ctrl+F or Ctrl+right arrow key
Move cursor left one word.	Ctrl+A or Ctrl+left arrow key
Move cursor to end of line.	Ctrl+QD or End
Move cursor to beginning of line.	Ctrl+QS
Place cursor on first line on screen at current column position.	Ctrl+QE
Place cursor on home line at first non-blank character.	Home Key
Move cursor down one line, keeping cursor at current column position.	Ctrl+X or down arrow key
Move cursor down one line to first character in next line.	Ctrl+J
Move cursor up one line.	Ctrl+E or up arrow key
Move cursor to bottom line of screen.	Ctrl+QX
Move cursor forward one page.	Ctrl+C or PgDn
Move cursor back one page.	Ctrl+R or PgUp
Move cursor right one page.	Ctrl+PgDn
Move cursor left one page.	Ctrl+PgUp
Move cursor to beginning of program.	Ctrl+Home or Ctrl+QR
Move cursor to end of program.	Ctrl+End or Ctrl+QC
Locate matching brace, parenthesis, or bracket.	Ctrl+]
Search for word or phrase.	Ctrl+QF
Go to first bookmark.	Ctrl+Q0
Go to second bookmark.	Ctrl+Q1
Go to third bookmark.	Ctrl+Q2
Go to fourth bookmark.	Ctrl+Q3

QuickC

Function	Keyboard Combination
Access menu bar.	Alt or F11
Cancel Help or a dialog box.	Esc

See also: Starting QuickC

Environment variables (accessing)

You can often increase a program's functionality by accessing the DOS environment variables. To do so, you can choose from several alternatives for your program. The first is to use the *envp* array. Each time you run a C program, DOS passes the *envp* array to *main()*. To access this array of pointers, declare *main()* as shown below:

```
main(int argc, char *argv[], char *envp[])
```

The *argc* and *argv* parameters let your programs access the command line arguments. Whether or not your program will use *argc* and *argv*, you must include *argc* and *argv* when you define *main()* if you plan to use the *envp* array.

The *envp* array is a NULL terminated list of character strings that contains the program's copy of the environment. The following program, called SHOWENV.C, uses the *envp* array to display the contents of the DOS environment:

```
/* SHOWENV.C */

#include <stdio.h>
main(int argc, char *argv[], char *envp[])
{
    int i;

    for (i = 0; envp[i] !=NULL; ++i)
        puts(envp[i]);
}
```

In the preceding example, the program displays each of the environment entries by using a *for* loop that terminates when the program encounters the terminating NULL.

The C run-time library provides the *getenv()* and *putenv()* functions that also allow your programs to access the DOS environment variables. The first function, *getenv()*, returns a pointer to the character string value that's associated with a specific environment variable.

For example, the following program displays the value that's associated with the PATH environment variable:

```
#include <stdio.h>
#include <stdlib.h>

main()
{
    char *value;

    value = getenv("PATH");

    if (value != NULL)
        printf("PATH=%s\n", value);
    else
        printf("PATH not defined\n");
}
```

If *getenv()* cannot locate an environment entry, the function returns the value NULL and the program prints a message to tell you that PATH is not defined.

The second function, *putenv()*, adds an entry to the program's copy of the environment. The following program creates an environment variable called FILE and assigns it the value TEST.DAT. The program then uses the *getenv()* function to display the variable's value:

```
#include <stdio.h>
#include <stdlib.h>

main()
{
    char *value;

    putenv("FILE=TEST.DAT");

    value = getenv("FILE");

    if (value != NULL)
        printf("FILE=%s\n", value);
    else
        printf("FILE not defined\n");
}
```

Each time you execute a program, DOS passes a copy of the current environment to that program. If the program changes environment variables or adds variables to the environment, the program makes those modifications to its own copy. When the program completes, the original environment remains unchanged. The only way to change an environment entry permanently is to use the DOS SET command.

See also: Command line (accessing), QuickC run-time library functions

Global variables and constants (predefined)

To help you develop your programs, QuickC predefines several global variables and constants. The following table summarizes them:

unsigned int _amblksiz
> The *_amblksiz* global variable specifies the size of the block of memory that memory-allocation functions such as *malloc()* and *calloc()* allocate. The first time you use these functions, they allocate a block of memory the size of *_amblksiz*, which is usually much larger than you requested. The memory-allocation functions meet the request for additional memory by parceling out available memory from this block. As a result, the functions reduce the number of memory-allocation calls—each of which is a slow process—to the operating system. The default size of *_amblksiz* is 8 KB. If you change the value of *_amblksiz*, you must do so in multiples of 2 KB. The malloc.h include file defines *_amblksiz*.

__DATE__
> The __DATE__ constant is defined as the date of compilation. Your program cannot change this constant's value.

int daylight
> The *daylight* variable indicates whether daylight saving time is in effect. If it is, *daylight* has a value of 1. If it is not, *daylight* has a value of 0. The value of *daylight* is determined by the value of the TZ environment variable. If TZ has not been set, the value of *daylight* is 1. The time.h include file declares *daylight*.

int _doserrno
> The *_doserrno* variable gives the DOS error code for the last system-level error that occurred. In general, you should access this variable to detect errors in operations that involve only input and output. Errors returned from other operations might not have an equivalent DOS error code. The stdlib.h include file declares *_doserrno*.

char *environ[]
> Each time you run a program, QuickC copies the DOS environment's current contents to the *environ* global

(continued)

variable. Each element of *environ* points to an environment variable and its value. Most programmers use the *getenv()* and *putenv()* run-time library functions to access the environment and to avoid directly accessing *environ*. The stdlib.h include file declares *environ*.

int errno Most C run-time library functions assign their error status values to the *errno* global variable. By examining the value of *errno*, your program can determine an error's cause and process accordingly. Refer to the C run-time library documentation for information about specific values that are assigned to *errno*. The stdlib.h include file declares *errno*.

__FILE__ The __FILE__ constant is defined as the current source filename. Your program cannot change this constant's value. You can change the value of this constant only during compilation by using the #line preprocessor directive.

int _fmode The *_fmode* variable specifies the default translation mode, whether text or binary. For QuickC, *_fmode* is set to text mode. To change to binary mode, set *_fmode* to the O_BINARY constant. Each time you use *fopen()* to open a file, you can specify the letter t or the letter b to set the access mode to text or binary translation. In text mode, the input and output functions translate the carriage return and line feed combination into line feeds on input and then reverse this process on output. In binary mode, this translation does not occur. If you do not specify a text or binary translation mode when you open a file, the routines examine the *_fmode* global variable. The stdlib.h include file declares *_fmode*.

__LINE__ The __LINE__ constant is defined as the current line number in the source file. You can change the value of this constant only during compilation by using the #line preprocessor directive.

unsigned char _osmajor
Each time you run a program, QuickC assigns the operating system's major version to the *_osmajor* global variable. In DOS 4.0, for example, this value is 4. The stdlib.h include file declares *_osmajor*.

unsigned char _osminor
Each time you run a program, QuickC assigns the operating system's minor version to the *_osminor* global variable. In DOS 4.0, for example, this value is 0. The stdlib.h include file declares *_osminor*.

unsigned int _osversion

> Each time you run a program, QuickC assigns the operating system's complete version number to the _osversion global variable. The low byte of _osversion contains the major version number, and the high byte contains the minor version number. In DOS 3.3, for example, _osversion contains the hexadecimal value 1f03. The decimal equivalent of 03 is 3, and the decimal equivalent of 1f is 30. The dos.h include file declares _osversion.

unsigned int _psp

> Each time you run a program, QuickC assigns the program segment prefix's (PSP) address to the _psp global variable. The program segment prefix contains such information as the command line, the address of the Ctrl+Break interrupt handler, and the address of the program's environment variables. The stdlib.h include file declares _psp.

__STDC__

> If your compiler enforces strict ANSI standards, the __STDC__ constant is defined as 1. The QuickC compiler does not enforce such standards, so __STDC__ has the value 0.

char *sys_errlist[]

> The *sys_errlist* global variable is an array of character string error messages. You can use the *errno* variable as an index to this array to access the error message that corresponds to a particular system error. The stdlib.h include file declares *sys_errlist* and the corresponding error messages.

int sys_nerr

> The *sys_errlist* array contains all the possible system error messages, and the *sys_nerr* global variable contains the number of error messages that are in that array.

__TIME__

> The __TIME__ constant is defined as the time of day that the program was compiled. Your program cannot change this constant's value.

__TIMESTAMP__

> The __TIMESTAMP__ constant is defined as the date-and-time stamp of the last modification to the program. Your program cannot change this constant's value.

long timezone
: The *timezone* variable contains the number of seconds by which the current time zone differs from Greenwich Mean Time. The value of *timezone* is determined by the TZ environment variable. If TZ has not been set, the value of *timezone* is 28800, which is the number of seconds in eight hours. The time.h include file declares *timezone*.

char *tzname[2]
: The first element in the *tzname* array is a character string that specifies the local time zone, such as PST or EST. The second element in *tzname* contains the daylight saving time zone name, such as PDT or EDT. The values in the array are determined by the TZ environment variable's value. If TZ has not been set, the first element of the *tzname* array is PST and the second is PDT. The time.h include file declares *tzname*.

See also: Environment variables (accessing), Preprocessor directives, QuickC run-time library functions

Help

QuickC provides detailed on-line help. To do so, QuickC keeps track of the current cursor position, making context-sensitive help possible as you edit your program. If you place the cursor on a C keyword such as *while* or *for* and press the F1 function key, QuickC displays a window of information about that subject. Likewise, if you place the cursor on a function name such as *printf()* or *fopen()*, pressing F1 displays a window of help for that function. QuickC displays general help information if you press the Shift+F1 keyboard combination.

The Contents and Index options are displayed at the top of the general help window. Select the Contents option and press Enter to display a list of help topics. To select a topic from the list, move the cursor to the topic you want and press either Enter or F1. QuickC displays information about that topic. To exit the help window and return to the editor, press the Esc key.

Select the Index option and press Enter to display a window of help topics that begin with the letter "a." QuickC also displays an alphabetic menu that you use to display topics that begin with the other letters of the alphabet. To display topics listed by a particular letter, press the letter on the keyboard and then press Enter. When the topic you want appears in the list, position the cursor on the topic and press

Enter to display QuickC's context-sensitive help for that topic. To return to the editor, press the Esc key.

When you select the Index or Contents option, QuickC displays the Notes option at the top of the screen. This option allows you to view the contents of an ASCII text file named NOTES.HLP. Using any editor, you can edit this file to create your own help notes. After you save the NOTES.HLP file, your notes are readily available whenever you choose the Index and Notes options from the help screen. To return from the NOTES.HLP file to the help screen, press Alt+F1.

In-line assembly language

A goal in any programming project is to write much of the program in a high-level language such as C. In some cases, however, you might need a small assembly language routine either to interface to specific hardware or to perform fast video output. QuickC lets you place in-line assembly language code fragments in your program. To do so, you must create an assembly language block, which is formatted as shown below:

```
_asm
{
    assembly language statements
}
```

If you do not use braces to group your assembly language statements when you create an assembly language block, you must precede each assembly language statement with the _asm keyword, as shown below:

```
_asm    mov   ah, 4
_asm    mov   dl, 65
_asm    int   21H
```

QuickC lets you use the general-purpose registers AX, BX, CX, and DX freely within your assembly language code. You must, however, preserve the value of the BP and SP base-pointer and stack-pointer registers. And you should be cautious if you use the DI and SI registers. QuickC uses these registers to store variables that are declared with the *register* keyword, so using DI and SI would alter the values of the variables.

QuickC does not restrict your assembly language blocks only to assembly language. In fact, QuickC lets you reference C constants, variables, labels, functions, and macros within an assembly language block. The following program, for example, uses a BIOS service to output the letters of the alphabet to your screen:

```
main()
{
    int letter, row = 10, column = 0;

    for (letter = 'A'; letter <= 'Z'; letter++)

        {
        _asm
            {
            mov ah, 2           ; set cursor function
            mov bh, 0           ; video display page 0
            mov dh, row         ; row for output
            mov dl, column      ; column for output
            int 10h             ; set the cursor
                                ; position
            inc column          ; increment column
            mov ah, 9           ; display character
                                ; function
            mov al, letter      ; letter to display
            mov bl, 7           ; character attribute
            mov cx, 1           ; number of characters
                                ; to output
            int 10h             ; output the character
            }
        }
}
```

Keywords (predefined)

A keyword is a word that C reserves for special use, such as the word "for" to signify the repetition of commands in a *for* loop or the word "if" for a conditional statement. Because C reserves its keywords for its own use, you cannot use those keywords as function or variable names. The following is a list of C's keywords:

auto	default	float	interrupt	signed	unsigned
break	do	for	long	sizeof	void
case	double	fortran	near	static	volatile
cdecl	else	goto	pascal	struct	while
char	enum	huge	register	switch	_export
const	extern	if	return	typedef	_loadds
continue	far	int	short	union	_saveregs

Libraries

Programmers often use the LIB utility to place commonly used functions in an object file library. Then the linker can access the library's contents to include those common functions that your program uses. To use a library file in QuickC, compile and link using a program list. The program list specifies every file that's needed to create the executable file. The following example demonstrates how to create a library.

To begin, create two files named TOUPR.C and TOLWR.C that contain the following functions:

```
/* toupr.c */

void string_to_uppercase(char *s)
{
    while(*s)
        {
        if(*s >= 'a' && *s <= 'z')
            *s -= 'a' - 'A';
        s++;
        }
}

/* tolwr.c */

void string_to_lowercase(char *s)
{
    while(*s)
        {
        if(*s >= 'A' && *s <= 'Z')
            *s += 'a' - 'A';
        s++;
        }
}
```

Next, using the Compile File command from the Make menu, compile the two source files to create object files.

Using the LIB utility from the command line, create the library file STRTO.LIB:

```
C> LIB

Microsoft (R) Library Manager  Version 3.14
Copyright (C) Microsoft Corp 1983-1989. All rights
reserved.
```

(continued)

```
Library name:STRTO.LIB
Library does not exist. Create? (y/n) Y
Operations:+TOUPR+TOLWR
List file:

C>
```

After you create the library file, enter the QuickC environment and create and save a file named TESTLIB.C that contains the following code:

```
/* testlib.c */

main()
{
    static char *str = "This is a test";

    string_to_lowercase(str);
    puts(str);
    string_to_uppercase(str);
    puts(str);
}
```

Next choose the Set Program List command from the Make menu to create a program list. QuickC displays a dialog box in which you type the name of the program list file. Type *TESTLIB.MAK* in the File Name box for this example, and press Enter. QuickC asks whether you want to create the file. After you click the Yes button, QuickC displays the Edit Program List dialog box that prompts you to enter the names of the files used to build the executable program. Type the filename *TESTLIB.C* in the File Name box, and press Enter. Then type the library filename *STRTO.LIB*, and press Enter. Select the Save List option, and press Enter. Choose the Build Program command from the Make menu. QuickC compiles and links the files that you specified in the program list. After the build operation completes, choose the Go command (F5) to execute the program.

See also: Compiling

Menus

You use convenient pull-down menus to choose commands in QuickC. As you edit your program in the QuickC environment, you can quickly access these menus by using the Alt key. Each time you press and release the Alt key when you work in the editor in QuickC (Alt+M if you are using the Microsoft editor), QuickC activates the menu bar.

(Note that you do not need to hold down the Alt key.) To select a specific menu, press the highlighted letter that corresponds to the menu. After QuickC displays a menu, you choose a command either by pressing the key that corresponds to a highlighted letter or by using the arrow keys to highlight a command and then pressing Enter. If you decide not to choose a command, press the Alt key a second time or the Esc key to deactivate the menu bar. To display a complete set of menus, choose the Full Menus command from the Options menu. The following sections briefly explain the commands that the menus include.

File menu

New	Clears the editing screen so that you can edit a new file
Open	Opens an existing file for editing
Open Last File	Opens the last file edited
Merge	Inserts the contents of another source file on the line that contains the cursor
Save	Saves the contents of the current file
Save As	Saves the contents of the current file to a new filename
Save All	Saves the contents of all modified files, such as the source, notepad, program list, and debug history files
Print	Prints the current contents of a file or of a selected range of text
DOS Shell	Exits QuickC temporarily so that you can execute DOS commands
Exit	Exits QuickC and returns to DOS

Edit menu

Undo	Reverses the most recent edit if the cursor is still on the edited line
Cut	Copies a block of text to the Clipboard and removes the text from the file
Copy	Copies a block of text to the Clipboard and leaves the text in the file
Paste	Copies the Clipboard contents to the current cursor position in the file
Clear	Erases a block of text from the file
Read Only	Marks the current file as read-only

View menu

Source
: Lets you select different source files (specified in the program list) in a multi-file edit

Include
: Displays the contents of an include file

Output Screen
: Toggles between the QuickC screen and the program output screen

Maximize
: Changes the current window from normal size to maximum size (full screen)

Windows
: Lets you open or close windows or toggle between windows that share the screen

Search menu

Find
: Searches an entire document for a specific word or phrase

Selected Text
: Searches for another occurrence of the currently highlighted text

Repeat Last Find
: Locates the next occurrence of a word or phrase used in the previous Find operation

Change
: Replaces one word or phrase with another

Function
: Finds the entry point of a function after you have compiled your program with debugging enabled

Next Error
: Displays the next syntax error that was found during compilation

Previous Error
: Displays the previous syntax error that was found during compilation

Make menu

Compile File
: Compiles the source file to an OBJ object file but does not link

Build Program
: Compiles and links all out-of-date files in a multi-module program

Rebuild All
: Compiles and links all files in a multi-module program

Set Program List
: Creates a program list file that defines the components of a multi-module program for rebuilding

Edit Program List
: Changes the contents of the program list

(continued)

Make menu *continued*

Clear Program List
    Removes the current program list from memory

Run menu

Restart   Sets execution to start at the beginning of the program

Go   Runs program or continues execution from the current statement if execution had been interrupted

Continue To Cursor
    Continues execution to the line that contains the cursor

Trace Into   Steps through the program, including function calls

Step Over   Steps through program execution, bypassing function calls

Animate   Highlights each statement as QuickC executes it

Debug menu

Calls   Displays the function calls that led to the current statement

Breakpoint   Lets you set a breakpoint location in the program, which will suspend execution and return control to you

Watchpoint   Lets you specify an expression that suspends execution when the expression is true

Watch Value   Lets you specify a variable whose name and value appear in the watch window

Modify Value   Lets you change a variable's value

History On   Creates or uses files that have the extension HIS or INP that contain a history of the debugging commands and the input typed at the keyboard during a debugging session

Undo   Backs up through debugging commands when History On is enabled

Replay   Replays all or a portion of a debugging session when History On is enabled

Truncate User Input
    Clears all the previous user input from a file that has the extension INP when History On is enabled

Utility menu

Run DOS Command
    Lets you execute a DOS command without exiting QuickC

Customize Menu
    Lets you add up to eight commands to the Utility menu

Learn QuickC Invokes the QuickC tutorial

Custom Editor Lets you select an editor other than the QuickC editor

Options menu

Display   Lets you select screen colors and define mouse options

Make   Lets you specify compiler and linker options

Run/Debug Lets you specify a command line for the program, control screen output, and choose what will be saved to a file during debugging

Environment Lets you define the subdirectories in which QuickC will search for include files, libraries, and on-line help

Full Menus Lets you toggle between full menus, which include all the debugging and program list commands, and short menus, which provide only those commands you need to get started with QuickC and develop programs that require only a single file

Help menu

Index   Displays an alphabetic list of topics

Contents   Displays a list of general help topics

Topic   Displays help about the keyword on which the cursor is positioned

Help on Help Displays information about help

See also: Compiling, Debugging, Help

Operators

All programming languages support the following mathematical operators for addition, subtraction, division, and multiplication: +, −, /, and ∗. The following tables define those operators and all others that C supports. A table later in this section shows the precedence of the operators, which determines the order in which operations are performed.

Arithmetic Operators

+	Addition
–	Subtraction
/	Division
*	Multiplication
%	Modulus (remainder)

Relational Operators

<	Less than
>	Greater than
<=	Less than or equal to
>=	Greater than or equal to
==	Equal to
!=	Not equal to

Logical Operators

&&	Logical AND
||	Logical OR
!	Logical NOT

Bitwise Operators

&	Bitwise AND
|	Bitwise OR
<<	Bit shift left
>>	Bit shift right
^	Bitwise exclusive OR
~	Bitwise complement

Assignment Operators

+=	Example: a += 5; is equal to a = a + 5;
–=	Example: a –= 5; is equal to a = a – 5;
*=	Example: a *= 3; is equal to a = a * 3;
/=	Example: a /= 3; is equal to a = a / 3;
%=	Example: a %= 2; is equal to a = a % 2;
<<=	Example: a <<= 3; is equal to a = a << 3;
>>=	Example: a >>= 2; is equal to a = a >> 2;
=	C assignment operator
^=	Example: a ^= 3; is equal to a = a ^ 3;
&=	Example: a &= 5; is equal to a = a & 5;
|=	Example: a |= 3; is equal to a = a | 3;

Increment and Decrement Operators

++	Example: x = a++; is equal to x = a; a = a + 1;
++	Example: x = ++a; is equal to a = a + 1; x = a;
––	Example: x = a––; is equal to x = a; a = a – 1;
––	Example: x = ––a; is equal to a = a – 1; x = a;

Miscellaneous Operators

sizeof	Returns the size of an object in bytes
,	Separates the variable initializations or the increments in a *for* loop
(*type*)	Forces type coercion (Cast operator)
.	Separates a structure name from a member name
->	Separates a structure name from a member name when pointers to the structure are used
()	Contains the parameters in a function call or groups an expression
[]	Specifies an offset from a pointer address (array index)
?:	Separates the expressions in a conditional statement (conditional assignment operator)
*	Gives the value at the address of a pointer (indirection operator for pointer references)
&	Gives the machine address of a pointer

To ensure that expression evaluation is consistent, C assigns a precedence order to its operators. Operators that have the highest precedence are performed first. If two operators that have the same precedence are in the same expression, C executes the operators in the expression from left to right or right to left, based on the specified associativity:

Operators	Highest Precedence Associativity	Operators	Highest Precedence Associativity
(), [], ., ->	left to right	^	left to right
!, ++, --, ~, -, (type), *, &, sizeof	right to left	|	left to right
		&&	left to right
*, /, %	left to right	||	left to right
+, -	left to right	?:	right to left
>>, <<	left to right	=, +=, -=, %=, *=, /=, <<=, >>=, ^=, &=, |=	right to left
>, <, >=, <=	left to right		
==, !=	left to right		
&	left to right	,	left to right

Pragmas

A pragma is a compiler directive. Because each pragma is specific to the C compiler implementation, a pragma might be available for only certain C compilers. In fact, QuickC supports only four pragmas, which are described in this section: check_stack, message, pack, and check_pointer.

The check_stack pragma

The check_stack pragma enables or disables stack checking for each function call. Each time your program calls a function, the program by default calls a routine that first checks to see if sufficient stack space exists for the function's parameters and local variables. If the routine finds enough stack space, the function is executed. If the routine does not find enough stack space, a stack overflow error occurs. The compiler adds the code for stack checking to the executable file during compilation. Although stack checking is important as you develop and test your program, you can eliminate the overhead of stack checking with each function call when your program is ready for production. Eliminating stack checking at that point improves your program's performance.

The /Gs compiler switch lets you disable stack checking for all the functions in the module you compile. In some cases, however, you might want to enable and disable stack checking on a function-by-function basis. The check_stack pragma allows you to do just that. The following pragma enables stack checking:

```
#pragma check_stack(on)
```

And the pragma below disables stack checking:

```
#pragma check_stack(off)
```

By placing this pragma before a specific function, you can enable or disable stack checking for that function.

The message pragma

The message pragma directs the compiler to send a message to stdout during compilation without generating a syntax error. The following is an example of the message pragma:

```
#pragma message("Link with GRAPHICS.LIB")
```

That example pragma would produce the following message when you compile the program that contains the pragma:

```
Link with GRAPHICS.LIB
```

The message pragma does not generate a syntax error, so it does not interrupt compilation.

The pack pragma

The pack pragma lets you specify the size of the boundaries in which to store each structure.

When the QuickC compiler allocates space for structures, it follows the rules below:

- Members of the *char* and *unsigned char* types and arrays of the *char* and *unsigned char* types are aligned by byte.
- Members of all other types are aligned by word.
- Structures are aligned by word. If a structure does not contain the even number of bytes required to fill a word, the compiler pads the structure so that it uses the whole word.

To conserve memory, you might occasionally want the QuickC compiler to pack structures into the least amount of space required. The /Zp command-line compiler option lets you specify the byte boundary in which to pack each structure in a module. The /Zp1 option uses a single-byte boundary, /Zp2 uses two bytes, and /Zp4 uses four bytes. The pack pragma lets you specify the padding for structures on an individual basis. For example, the following pragma would direct QuickC to pack the structures on a double-byte boundary:

```
#pragma pack(2)
```

Keep in mind that packing structures might slow program execution because a structure must be unpacked each time it is referenced.

The check_pointer pragma

The check_pointer pragma enables or disables checking for NULL or out-of-range pointers. If you compile your program using the /Zr command-line compiler option or the Pointer Check option in QuickC, the QuickC compiler checks your program for NULL or out-of-range pointers. If the compiler encounters such a pointer, it generates an error. The check_pointer pragma lets you enable or disable pointer checking throughout the program, regardless of whether you used the /Zr or Pointer Check option. For example, the following pragma enables pointer checking:

```
#pragma check_pointer(on)
```

And the following pragma disables pointer checking:

```
#pragma check_pointer(off)
```

After you test your program thoroughly, disable pointer checking to speed your program's performance.

See also: Compiling

Preprocessor directives

C supports several preprocessor directives. These directives are commands to the compiler that are performed before the compiler creates the executable code. C supports the following preprocessor directives, which are described in this section: #define, #undef, #include, #if, #elif, #else, #endif, #ifdef, #ifndef, #error, #line, and #pragma.

The #define and #undef directives

The #define directive lets you define constants and macros. During preprocessing of a program, the compiler replaces every instance of the constant or macro name with its definition. The #undef directive removes ("undefines") the definition of a previously defined constant or macro. The following examples demonstrate how to use the #define directive:

```
#define NUM_STUDENTS 100    /*sets the number
                              of students to 100*/
#define inch_to_cm(x) ((x) * 2.54)
                            /*converts x from
                              inches to centimeters */
```

If, later in your program, you want to create a more elaborate function to perform an inch-to-centimeter conversion, undefine the *inch_to_cm* macro by using the #undef directive as follows:

```
#undef inch_to_cm
```

The #undef directive shown above undefines the *inch_to_cm* macro from the point at which the directive is placed in the program to the program's end.

The #include directive

The #include directive tells the preprocessor to insert the specified file in your source file for compilation with your program. This directive takes either of the following formats:

```
#include <filename>
#include "pathname\filename"
```

In the first of the two preceding directives, the brackets <> direct the preprocessor to search for the file in the subdirectories that are specified by the INCLUDE environment variable. If the preprocessor cannot find the file in the specified subdirectories, it searches the current directory. The brackets are usually used to include files that the C compiler provides.

If you specify an include filename within quotation marks, as in the second of the preceding directives, the preprocessor searches for the file in the subdirectory that's specified in the pathname; or, it searches the current directory if only a filename is specified. If the preprocessor does not find the file, it searches the subdirectories specified by the INCLUDE environment variable.

Conditional directives: #if, #elif, #else, and #endif

The preprocessor supports a set of directives that let you perform conditional preprocessing. The following is a list of these directives:

- #if—Tests the specified expression. If the expression is true, the preprocessor includes the statements that follow, up to an #endif, #else, or #elif directive.

- #elif—Works like an else-if statement, allowing you to test another expression if the expressions that follow the #if directive, and any previous #elif directive, were false. If the specified expression is true, the preprocessor includes the statements that follow the #elif directive, up to an #endif, #else, or #elif directive.

- #else—Allows you to provide a set of statements that the preprocessor includes if none of the preceding conditions are met.

- #endif—Marks the end of a set of conditional directives. After one of the expressions that follow a directive is found to be true and the statements that follow the directive are included for compilation, the preprocessor skips to the #endif directive and continues processing from that point.

The ANSI standard for C supports the *defined* macro, which returns a value of true (nonzero) if the specified identifier is defined, or false (0) if the identifier is undefined. For example, the following statements determine the specific operating system and then print an appropriate comment:

```
#if defined(MSDOS)
    printf("Running MS-DOS\n");
#elif defined(OS_2)
    printf("Running OS/2\n");
#elif defined(UNIX)
    printf("Running UNIX\n");
#else
    printf("Operating system is unknown\n");
#endif
```

The #if and #elif directives can also examine standard C expressions such as the following:

```
#if (sizeof(int) == 4)
```

By using the C NOT operator (!), you can reverse the logic of an #if directive, as shown below:

```
#if !defined(MSDOS)
    printf("Not running MS-DOS\n");
```

The #ifdef and #ifndef directives

The #ifdef directive tells the preprocessor to include the code that follows, up to the #endif statement, only if the specified identifier is defined. The #ifndef directive, however, tells the preprocessor to include the code only if the specified identifier is not defined.

Using these directives is the same as using the #if directive followed by the *defined* macro. For example, the following two statements are functionally equivalent:

```
#ifdef DEBUG
#if defined(DEBUG)
```

Similarly, if you use the C NOT operator (!) with *defined*, the two statements below are functionally equivalent:

```
#ifndef DEBUG
#if !defined(DEBUG)
```

Programmers often use the #ifdef and #ifndef directives during debugging.

Consider this scenario: You have placed several *printf* statements for debugging within your functions. Rather than having to comment out or remove the *printf* statements from your functions when the code is working, you can use the #ifdef directive. For instance, review the example on the following page.

```c
int sum_array(int array[], int num_elements)
{
    int sum = 0;
    int i;

    for(i = 0; i < num_elements; i++)
        {
#ifdef DEBUG
        printf("%d %d\n", sum, array[i]);
#endif
        sum += array[i];
        }
        return(sum);
}
```

In the above example, the preprocessor includes the *printf* statement if the DEBUG identifier is defined. If DEBUG is not defined, the preprocessor does not include the *printf* statement.

If you are debugging several functions in your program, you can use #define and #undef to enable the debug messages for some functions and disable the debug messages for others, as the example below shows:

```c
#define DEBUG 1

void display(int array[], int num_elements)
{
    /* statements for displaying */

#ifdef DEBUG
    printf("In the display function\n");
#endif
}

#undef DEBUG /* turn off debug write */

int sum_array(int array[], int num_elements)
{
    int sum = 0;
    int i;

    for(i = 0; i < num_elements; ++i)
        {
#ifdef DEBUG
        printf("%d %d\n", sum, array[i]);
#endif
        sum += array[i];
        }
}
```

In the preceding example, the program enables the *printf* debug messages for the *display()* function but disables them for the *sum_array()* function. If you wanted to enable the messages for *sum_array()*, you would remove the #undef DEBUG statement that precedes the function and then recompile.

As you can see from the preceding example, the #endif directive groups the statements that are associated with the #ifdef or #ifndef directive. After the preprocessor encounters an #ifdef or #ifndef directive, it conditionally compiles the statements that are included between the directive and the #endif.

The #error directive

The #error directive tells the preprocessor to generate the specified syntax error message. For example, review the following directive:

```
#error Compile this program with /Ox
```

This directive generates the following compiler error message:

```
test.c(1): error C2188: #error : Compile this
program with /Ox
```

In the above example, "test.c" is the name of the source file, "(1)" is the line number on which the error occurred, and "C2188" is the error code associated with the error that the #error directive generated.

Many programmers use the #error directive to generate an error when a specific identifier is undefined.

The #line directive

The #line directive instructs the preprocessor to set its internal line counter and filename to the specified constant and name. For example, the following directive sets the line counter to 100:

```
#line 100
```

Each time the compiler locates a syntax error, the compiler displays the number of the line that contains the error. By setting the line counter to a specific value prior to compiling each function, you can use the #line directive to locate errors.

The #line directive also lets you specify the filename that is displayed when the compiler displays a syntax error message. Assume that the compiler locates a syntax error on the fifth line after the directive that is shown below:

```
#line 100 "String Copy Function"
```

The compiler then displays the following syntax error message, which might help you locate the syntax error quickly:

```
String Copy Function(105) : error C2143:
syntax error : missing ';' before 'div op'
```

The #pragma directive

The #pragma directive allows you to use a set of compiler directives that are specific to each C compiler implementation.

See also: Debugging, Pragmas

printf control sequences

The most commonly used C function is probably *printf()*. The following table summarizes the *printf* escape sequences:

Escape Sequence	*Function*	*Escape Sequence*	*Function*
\a	Sounds computer's bell	\v	Vertical tab
		\'	Single quotation mark
\b	Backspace	\"	Double quotation mark
\f	Formfeed	\\	Backslash
\n	New line	\nnn	ASCII character in octal
\r	Carriage return	\xnn	ASCII character in hexadecimal
\t	Horizontal tab		

In addition to the escape sequences shown above, C supports a collection of format specifiers that dictate the output format. The following table summarizes the format specifiers that *printf* supports:

Format Specifier	*Output*
%d	Decimal integer
%i	Decimal integer
%u	Unsigned decimal integer
%o	Unsigned octal integer
%x	Unsigned hexadecimal integer, lowercase letters
%X	Unsigned hexadecimal integer, uppercase letters
%f	Fixed-point value of the float type
%e	Scientific notation with a lowercase e
%E	Scientific notation with an uppercase E
%g	%e or %f, whichever is shorter
%G	%E or %F, whichever is shorter
%c	ASCII character
%s	Character string
%p	Pointer value

You can place a type prefix before the format specifier to further describe the type that *printf* will print. The following table shows the type prefixes:

Type Prefix	*Type Printed*
F	Far pointer
N	Near pointer
h	Short integer
l	Long integer or double
L	Long double

The *printf* function also lets you include width and precision values and justification flags in the *printf* statement. The plus sign in a format specifier directs *printf* to precede the value with its sign (+ or −). A minus sign in a format specifier directs *printf* to display the value as left justified. By default, *printf* displays each value as right justified. The complete format specification looks like the following:

%[flags][width][.precision][type prefix]format type

The following *printf* statements contain valid format specifications:

```
printf("%d %3d %i %f %5.2f\n", 3, 3, 3, 2.713, 2.713);
printf("%+d\t%-3d\n", 2, 5);
```

Types

Variables store values when your program executes, and each of those variables must be a specific type. A variable's type determines the set of values that the variable can store and the set of operations that can be performed on the variable.

C supports five basic types; these are *int*, *float*, *char*, *double*, and *enum*. In addition, QuickC provides several type qualifiers that change the range of values a type can store, including the *long*, *short*, *signed,* and *unsigned* qualifiers. The following table illustrates the range of values that each C data type can store:

Type	*Range of Values*
char, signed char	$1MI128 through 127
unsigned char	0 through 255
int, signed, signed int	−32,768 through 32,767
short int, short, signed short, signed short int	−32,768 through 32,767
unsigned int, unsigned	0 through 65,535

Type	*Range of Values*
unsigned short int, unsigned short	0 through 65,535
enum	0 through 65,535
long int, long, signed long, signed long int	−2,147,483,648 through 2,147,483,647
unsigned long int, unsigned long	0 to 4,294,967,295
float	3.48E(+−)38 (7 digits of precision)
double	1.7E(+−)308 (15 digits of precision)
long double	1.7E(+−)308 (15 digits of precision)

In addition to the long, short, signed, and unsigned qualifiers, C supports several storage class modifiers that specify how the program will store a variable in memory, as explained below:

- *auto*—States that the variable is local to the current block of code. When the code begins, the variable is created on the stack. When the code completes, the variable is removed from the stack. The auto modifier is the default for C variables.

- *const*—States that while the program executes the variable's value cannot be changed.

- *extern*—States that the variable is static in scope (i.e., not automatic) and is declared outside the current module.

- *register*—States that, to improve the program's performance, the compiler will use a register to store the variable's value. Using the *register* keyword does not guarantee that the value will reside in a register permanently, but that the compiler will store the value in a register when possible.

- *static*—States that the variable is global, and so will retain its value from one function call to the next. The scope of the variable is the file in which it's declared if the variable is declared externally from the functions in the file. If the variable is declared in a block of code, its scope is the block.

- *void*—States that the pointer to memory is not a specific type. If void is used in a function's declaration, void states that the function does not return a value or that it accepts no arguments.

- *volatile*—States that, while the program executes, the variable can be changed at any time. The variable change can come from the program or from an outside source, such as an interrupt.

3: *QuickC Libraries and Functions*

QuickC include files and the functions they contain

QuickC provides a large collection of include files that contain macro and type definitions, as well as function declarations. The following list briefly describes the contents of QuickC's include files. The list also shows the functions that are declared and the macros that are defined in the file.

ASSERT.H
Contains the assert debugging macro
assert()

BIOS.H
Contains function declarations for the BIOS services

_bios_disk()	_bios_equiplist()	_bios_keybrd()
_bios_memsize()	_bios_printer()	_bios_serialcom()
_bios_timeofday()	int86()	int86x()

CONIO.H
Contains function declarations for the console and port functions

cgets()	cprintf()	cputs()
cscanf()	getch()	getche()
inp()	inpw()	kbhit()
outp()	outpw()	putch()
ungetch()		

CTYPE.H
Contains character classification macros

isalnum()	isalpha()	isascii()
iscntrl()	isdigit()	isgraph()
islower()	isprint()	ispunct()
isspace()	isupper()	isxdigit()
outpw()	putch()	toascii()
tolower()	_tolower()	toupper()
_toupper()	ungetch()	

DIRECT.H
Contains function declarations for directory manipulation routines

chdir()	getcwd()	mkdir()
rmdir()		

DOS.H
Contains function declarations for the DOS system services

bdos()	_chain_intr()	_disable()
_dos_allocmem()	_dos_close()	_dos_creat()
_dos_creatnew()	dosexterr()	_dos_findfirst()
_dos_findnext()	_dos_freemem()	_dos_getdate()
_dos_getdiskfree()	_dos_getdrive()	_dos_getfileattr()
_dos_getftime()	_dos_gettime()	_dos_getvect()
_dos_keep()	_dos_open()	_dos_read()
_dos_setblock()	_dos_setdate()	_dos_setdrive()
_dos_setfileattr()	_dos_setftime()	_dos_settime()
_dos_setvect()	_dos_write()	_enable()
FP_OFF()	FP_SEG()	_harderr()
_hardresume()	_hardretn()	int86()
int86x()	intdos()	intdosx()
segread()		

ERRNO.H
Contains error definitions for values assigned to *errno*

FCNTL.H
Contains constants used by *open()* and *sopen()*

FLOAT.H
Contains constants and function declarations for floating-point math functions

_clear87()	_control87()	_fpreset()
_status87()		

GRAPH.H
Contains function declarations for graphics and font functions

_arc()	_clearscreen()	_displaycursor()
_ellipse()	_floodfill()	_getactivepage()
_getbkcolor()	_getcolor()	_getcurrentposition()
_getfillmask()	_getfontinfo()	_getgtextextent()
_getimage()	_getlinestyle()	_getphyscoord()
_getpixel()	_gettextcolor()	_gettextcursor()
_gettextposition()	_getvideoconfig()	_getviewcoord()
_getvisualpage()	_getwindowcoord()	_imagesize()
_lineto()	_moveto()	_outgtext()
_outtext()	_pie()	_putimage()
_rectangle()	_registerfonts()	_remapallpalette()
_remappalette()	_selectpalette()	_setactivepage()
_setbkcolor()	_setcliprgn()	_setcolor()
_setfillmask()	_setfont()	_setlinestyle()
_setpixel()	_settextcolor()	_settextcursor()
_settextposition()	_settextrows()	_settextwindow()
_setvideomode()	_setvideomoderows()	_setvieworg()
_setviewport()	_setvisualpage()	_setwindow()
_unregisterfonts()	_wrapon()	

IO.H
Contains function declarations for low-level file handling and I/O functions

access()	chmod()	chsize()
close()	creat()	dup()
dup2()	eof()	filelength()
isatty()	locking()	lseek()
mktemp()	open()	read()
remove()	rename()	setmode()
sopen()	tell()	umask()
unlink()	write()	

LIMITS.H
Contains the limits (range) of values that each C type can store

MALLOC.H
Contains function declarations for memory-allocation routines

alloca()	calloc()	_expand()
_ffree()	_fheapchk()	_fheapset()
_fheapwalk()	_fmalloc()	_fmsize()
free()	_freect()	halloc()
_heapchk()	_heapset()	_heapwalk()
hfree()	malloc()	_memavl()
_memmax()	_msize()	_nfree()
_nheapchk()	_nheapset()	_nheapwalk()
_nmalloc()	_nmsize()	realloc()
sbrk()	stackavail()	

MATH.H
Contains function declarations for mathematic functions

abs()	acos()	asin()
atan()	atan2()	atof()
cabs()	ceil()	cos()
cosh()	dieeetomsbin()	dmsbintoieee()
exp()	fabs()	fieeetomsbin()
floor()	fmod()	fmsbintoieee()
frexp()	hypot()	j0()
j1()	jn()	labs()
ldexp()	log()	log10()
matherr()	modf()	pow()
sin()	sinh()	sqrt()
tan()	tanh()	y0()
y1()	yn()	

MEMORY.H
Contains function declarations for buffer-manipulation routines

memccpy()	memchr()	memcmp()
memcpy()	memicmp()	memset()
movedata()		

PGCHART.H
Contains constants and function declarations for presentation graphics routines

_pg_analyzechart()	_pg_analyzechartms()	_pg_analyzepie()
_pg_analyzescatter()	_pg_analyzescatterms()	_pg_chart()
_pg_chartms()	_pg_chartpie()	_pg_chartscatter()
_pg_chartscatterms()	_pg_defaultchart()	_pg_getchardef()
_pg_getpalette()	_pg_getstyleset()	_pg_hlabelchart()
_pg_initchart()	_pg_resetpalette()	_pg_resetstyleset()
_pg_setchardef()	_pg_setpalette()	_pg_setstyleset()
_pg_vlabelchart()		

PROCESS.H
Contains function declarations for process control routines

abort()	execl()	execle()
execlp()	execlpe()	execv()
execve()	execvp()	execvpe()
exit()	_exit()	getpid()
spawnl()	spawnle()	spawnlp()
spawnlpe()	spawnv()	spawnve()
spawnvp()	spawnvpe()	system()

SEARCH.H
Contains function declarations for searching and sorting

bsearch()	lfind()	lsearch()
qsort()		

SETJMP.H
Contains function declarations for the *setjmp()* and *longjmp()* functions

longjmp()   setjmp()

SHARE.H
Contains constants used for file sharing by sopen

SIGNAL.H
Contains function declarations for signaling and constants used for string manipulation

raise()   signal()

STDARG.H
Contains macros used to access parameters in functions that support a variable number of parameters

va_arg()   va_end()   va_start()

STDDEF.H
Contains standard definitions and declarations for constants, types, and variables

STDIO.H
Contains function declarations and macros for the standard I/O functions

clearerr()	fclose()	fcloseall()
fdopen()	feof()	ferror()
fflush()	fgetc()	fgetchar()
fgetpos()	fgets()	fileno()
flushall()	fopen()	fprintf()
fputc()	fputchar()	fputs()

(continued)

fread()	freopen()	fscanf()
fseek()	fsetpos()	ftell()
fwrite()	getc()	getchar()
gets()	getw()	perror()
printf()	putc()	putchar()
puts()	putw()	remove()
rename()	rewind()	rmtmp()
scanf()	setbuf()	setvbuf()
sprintf()	sscanf()	tempnam()
tmpfile()	tmpnam()	ungetc()
unlink()	vfprintf()	vprintf()
vsprintf()		

STDLIB.H
Contains function declarations for common run-time library routines

abort()	abs()	atexit()
atof()	atoi()	atol()
bsearch()	calloc()	div()
ecvt()	exit()	_exit()
fcvt()	free()	gcvt()
getenv()	itoa()	labs()
ldiv()	_lrotl()	_lrotr()
ltoa()	_makepath()	malloc()
max()	min()	onexit()
perror()	putenv()	qsort()
rand()	realloc()	_rotl()
_rotr()	_searchenv()	_splitpath()
srand()	strtod()	strtol()
strtoul()	swab()	system()
tolower()	toupper()	ultoa()

STRING.H
Contains function declarations for string-manipulation routines

memccpy()	memchr()	memcmp()
memcpy()	memicmp()	memmove()
memset()	movedata()	strcat()
strchr()	strcmp()	strcmpi()
strcpy()	strcspn()	strdup()
strerror()	_strerror()	stricmp()
strlen()	strlwr()	strncat()
strncmp()	strncpy()	strnicmp()
strnset()	strpbrk()	strrchr()
strrev()	strset()	strspn()
strstr()	strtok()	strupr()

SYS\LOCKING.H
Contains constants used by the *locking()* function

SYS\STAT.H
Contains function declarations and structure definitions used by the file-status routines

fstat()   stat()

SYS\TIMEB.H
Contains the function declaration and structures used by the *ftime()* function

ftime()

SYS\TYPES.H
Contains file-status and time types

SYS\UTIME.H
Contains the function declaration and structure used by the *utime()* function

utime()

TIME.H
Contains function declarations for time manipulation routines

asctime()	clock()	ctime()
difftime()	gmtime()	localtime()
mktime()	_strdate()	_strtime()
time()	tzset()	

VARARGS.H
Contains macros used to access parameters in functions that support a variable number of parameters

va_arg()   va_end()   va_start()

QuickC run-time library functions

The following is a list of the QuickC run-time library functions. Each entry includes the function's name, its syntax, the include file or files in which it resides, and a short description.

abort
Syntax: void abort(void);
Include files: <process.h>, <stdlib.h>
Terminates the current program, displays an error message, and returns an error status value of 3.

abs
Syntax: int abs(int *expression*);
Include files: <stdlib.h>, <math.h>
Returns the absolute value of an integer expression.

access
Syntax: int access(char *pathname*, int *access_mode*);
Include file: <io.h>
Determines whether a file with the path and name given by *pathname* exists on disk and if the program can access that file in the mode. If so, *access()* returns a value of 0. The question that *access()* addresses depends on the value of the *access_mode* parameter, as shown in the following table:

access_mode	Question
0	Does the file exist as specified?
2	Can the file be accessed for write operations?
4	Can the file be accessed for read operations?
6	Can the file be accessed for read and write operations?

acos
Syntax: double acos(double *expression*);
Include file: <math.h>
Returns the arccosine of a numeric expression.

alloca
Syntax: void *alloca(size_t *num_bytes*);
Include file: <malloc.h>
Allocates the number of specified bytes from the program's stack space, and returns a void pointer to the memory space.

_arc
Syntax: short far _arc(short *x_left*, short *y_top*, short *x_right*, short *y_bottom*, short *x_start*, short *y_start*, short *x_stop*, short *y_stop*);
Include file: <graph.h>
Draws an elliptical arc. The center of the arc is at the center of the rectangle defined by the points (*x_left*, *y_top*) and (*x_right*, *y_bottom*). The arc starts at the point (*x_start*, *y_start*) and ends at (*x_stop*, *y_stop*).

asctime
Syntax: char *asctime(struct tm *datetime*);
Include file: <time.h>
Uses the members of the structure *datetime*, which contains a date and time, to create a 26-character string that includes the date and time. For member names, see the include file *time.h*.

asin
Syntax: double asin(double *expression*);
Include file: <math.h>
Returns the arcsine of a numeric expression.

assert
Syntax: void assert(int *expression*);
Include file: <assert.h>
Tests an expression that ends the program by calling the *abort()* function if the *expression* is false.

atan
Syntax: double atan(double *expression*);
Include file: <math.h>
Returns the arctangent of a numeric expression.

atan2
Syntax: double atan2(double *y*, double *x*);
Include file: <math.h>
Returns the arctangent of the numeric expression specified by y/x.

atexit
Syntax: int atexit(void(*function*)(void));
Include file: <stdlib.h>
Adds a function to the list of functions (up to 32) that C executes when the program completes its execution.

atof, atoi, atol
Syntax: double atof(const char *str*);
Syntax: int atoi(const char *str*);
Syntax: long atol(const char *str*);
Include file: <stdlib.h>
Converts a character string to the corresponding floating-point (atof), integer (atoi), or long (atol) value. The function *atof()* is also found in the math.h include file.

bdos
Syntax: int bdos(int *dos_function*, unsigned int *dx_register*, unsigned int *al_register*);
Include file: <dos.h>
Executes the DOS system service specified by *dos_function* after placing *dx_register* and *al_register* in the DX and AL registers, respectively, and returns the value of the AX register.

Bessel Functions—j0, j1, jn, y0, y1, yn
Syntax: j0(double *expression*);   /* 0 order, 1st kind */
Syntax: j1(double *expression*);   /* 1st order, 1st kind */
Syntax: jn(int *order*, double *expression*); /* n order, 1st kind */
Syntax: y0(double *expression*);   /* 0 order, 2nd kind */
Syntax: y1(double *expression*);   /* 1st order, 2nd kind */
Syntax: yn(int *order*, double *expression*); /* n order, 2nd kind */
Include file: <math.h>
Returns first and second order Bessel functions of *expression*.

_bios_disk
Syntax: unsigned _bios_disk(unsigned *service*, struct diskinfo_t
            **diskinfo*);
Include file: <bios.h>
Uses BIOS interrupt 0x13 to access the disk services. For a list of disk services, see the bios.h file.

_bios_equiplist
Syntax: unsigned _bios_equiplist(void);
Include file: <bios.h>
Uses BIOS interrupt 0x11 to return a value whose bits indicate what hardware is present in the system:

Bit(s)	*Significance*
0	1 if a floppy-disk drive is installed
1	1 if a math coprocessor is installed
2–3	System board ram is installed
4–5	Initial video mode
	01 40x25
	10 80x25
	11 80x25 monochrome
6–7	Number of floppy-disk drives
	0 0 = 1
	0 1 = 2
	1 0 = 3
	1 1 = 4
8	0 if a DMA chip is installed
9–11	Number of serial ports
12	1 if a game adapter is installed
13	1 if a serial printer is installed
14–15	Number of attached printers

_bios_keybrd
Syntax: unsigned _bios_keybrd(unsigned *service*);
Include file: <bios.h>
Uses BIOS interrupt 0x16 to access the keyboard services. For a list of keyboard services, see the bios.h file.

_bios_memsize
Syntax: unsigned _bios_memsize(void);
Include file: <bios.h>
Uses BIOS interrupt 0x12 to return the amount of memory in 1 KB blocks.

_bios_printer
Syntax: unsigned _bios_printer(unsigned *service*, unsigned *printer_port*, unsigned *output_data*);
Include file: <bios.h>
Uses BIOS interrupt 0x17 to access the printer services. For a list of printer services, see the bios.h file.

_bios_serialcom
Syntax: unsigned _bios_serialcom(unsigned *service*, unsigned *serial_port*, unsigned *data*);
Include file: <bios.h>
Uses BIOS interrupt 0x14 to access the BIOS serial communication services. For a list of communication services, see the bios.h file.

_bios_timeofday
Syntax: unsigned _bios_timeofday(int *service*, long *clock_value*);
Include file: <bios.h>
Uses BIOS interrupt 0x1A to access the time-of-day services. For a list of time-of-day services, see the bios.h file.

bsearch
Syntax: void *bsearch(const void *key_element*, const void *base_address*, size_t *num_elements*, size_t *element_width*, int (**compare*)(const void *a*, const void *b*));
Include files: <search.h>, <stdlib.h>
Performs a binary search for the value of *key_element* in an array that is sorted in ascending order and specified by *base_address*. Your program must define the function *compare()*, which uses pointers to compare two values.

cabs
Syntax: double cabs(struct complex *complex_number*);
Include file: <math.h>
Returns the absolute value of a complex number with the following structure:

```
struct complex
    {
    double x;    /* real part */
    double y;    /* imaginary part */
    };
```

calloc
Syntax: void *calloc(size_t *num_elements*, size_t *element_size*);
Include files: <malloc.h>, <stdlib.h>
Allocates from the heap an amount of memory large enough to hold an array of *num_elements*, with each element *element_size* in size, and initializes each element to zero. Returns a void pointer to the start of the allocated memory location.

ceil
Syntax: double ceil(double *expression*);
Include file: <math.h>
Returns a value of type *double* that is the smallest integer greater than or equal to the expression.

cgets
Syntax: char *cgets(char *str*);
Include file: <conio.h>
Reads a string of characters directly from keyboard and stores it in *str*.

_chain_intr
Syntax: void _chain_intr(void(interrupt far *handler*)());
Include file: <dos.h>
Chains one interrupt handler to another.

chdir
Syntax: int chdir(char *pathname*);
Include file: <direct.h>
Changes the current directory to the one indicated by *pathname*.

chmod
Syntax: int chmod(char *pathname*, int *permission*);
Include file: <io.h>
Changes a file's access permission. If successful, *chmod()* returns a value of 0. The permissions are as follows:

S_IREAD	Read access only
S_IWRITE	Write access
S_IREAD ¦ S_IWRITE	Read and write access

chsize
Syntax: int chsize(int *handle*, long *new_size*);
Include file: <io.h>
Changes the size of a file that is associated with the given file handle. If successful, *chsize()* returns a value of 0.

_clear87
Syntax: unsigned int _clear87(void);
Include file: <float.h>
Clears the word that gives math coprocessor floating-point status and sets it to 0.

clearerr
Syntax: void clearerr(FILE *file_pointer);
Include file: <stdio.h>
Resets the error and end-of-file indicator flags for specified file to 0.

_clearscreen
Syntax: void far _clearscreen(short screen_area);
Include file: <graph.h>
Erases the screen, graphics viewport, or text window. The *screen_area* parameter specifies the region of the screen to be cleared:

_GCLEARSCREEN	Clears the entire screen display
_GVIEWPORT	Clears the graphics viewport
_GWINDOW	Clears the current text window

clock
Syntax: clock_t *clock*(void);
Include file: <time.h>
Returns the amount of processor time that the current process has consumed.

close
Syntax: int close(int *file_handle*);
Include file: <io.h>
Closes the file that is associated with the given file handle.

_control87
Syntax: unsigned int _control87(unsigned int *new_controlword*, unsigned int *control_mask*);
Include file: <float.h>
Returns the current math coprocessor floating-point control word and sets the control word to the indicated value in *control_mask*.

cos
Syntax: double cos(double *expression*);
Include file: <math.h>
Returns the cosine of a numeric expression.

cosh
Syntax: double cosh(double *expression*);
Include file: <math.h>
Returns the hyperbolic cosine of a numeric expression.

cprintf
Syntax: int cprintf(char *format_string*[,*output_data*...]);
Include file: <conio.h>
Writes formatted output directly to the console.

cputs
Syntax: int cputs(char *string*);
Include file: <conio.h>
Writes a null terminated (ASCIIZ) string to the console.

creat
Syntax: int creat(char *pathname*, int *permission*);
Include file: <io.h>
Creates a new file or erases the contents of an existing file on disk and returns a file handle to the file. If successful, the *creat()* function returns a value of 0. The *permission* parameter specifies the file's access permission:

S_IREAD	Read access only
S_IWRITE	Write access
S_IREAD ¦ S_IWRITE	Read and write access

cscanf
Syntax: int cscanf(char *format_string*[, *pointer_argument*...]);
Include file: <conio.h>
Reads data directly from the console to the specified variables.

ctime
Syntax: char *ctime(const time_t *seconds*);
Include file: <time.h>
Converts seconds since midnight of 01/01/1970 Greenwich time to a date/time string.

dieeetomsbin
Syntax: int dieeetomsbin(double *ieee*, double *msbin*);
Include file: <math.h>
Converts a double-precision value that is in IEEE format to Microsoft binary format.

difftime
Syntax: double difftime(time_t *finish_time*, time_t *start_time*);
Include file: <time.h>
Calculates in seconds the difference between two times.

_disable
Syntax: void _disable(void);
Include file: <dos.h>
Disables hardware interrupts until the _enable() function is called.

_displaycursor
Syntax: short far _displaycursor(short *on_or_off*);
Include file: <graph.h>
Specifies whether the run-time library graphics routines turn the cursor on or off when they complete. The value of *on_or_off* determines the result of the function call:

_GCURSORON	Turns cursor on
_GCURSOROFF	Turns cursor off

div
Syntax: struct div_t div(int *numerator*, int *denominator*);
Include file: <stdlib.h>
Divides the specified numerator by the denominator and returns a structure that contains a quotient and a remainder:

```
struct div_t
    {
    int quot;
    int rem;
    };
```

dmsbintoieee
Syntax: int dmsbintoieee(double *msbin*, double *ieee*);
Include file: <math.h>
Converts a double-precision value stored in Microsoft binary format to IEEE format.

_dos_allocmem
Syntax: unsigned _dos_allocmem(unsigned *paragraphs*, unsigned *segment*);
Include file: <dos.h>
Allocates memory using DOS system service 0x48.

_dos_close
Syntax: unsigned _dos_close(int *file_handle*);
Include file: <dos.h>
Uses DOS service 0x3E to close the file that's associated with the specified file handle.

_dos_creat
Syntax: unsigned _dos_creat(char *pathname*, unsigned *attribute*, int *file_handle*);
Include file: <dos.h>
Uses DOS service 0x3C to create a new file or erase the contents of the file if it already exists.

_dos_creatnew
Syntax: unsigned _dos_creatnew(char *pathname*, unsigned *attribute*, int *file_handle*);
Include file: <dos.h>
Uses DOS service 0x5B to create the specified file only if a file that has the same name does not exist on disk.

dosexterr
Syntax: int dosexterr(struct DOSERROR *error_info*);
Include file: <dos.h>
Uses DOS service 0x59 to return extended error information for a DOS error.

_dos_findfirst
Syntax: unsigned _dos_findfirst(char *pathname*, unsigned *attribute*, struct find_t *fileinfo*);
Include file: <dos.h>
Uses DOS service 0x4E to find information about the first file that matches the file specification given in a directory search.

_dos_findnext
Syntax: unsigned _dos_findnext(struct find_t *fileinfo*);
Include file: <dos.h>
Uses DOS service 0x4F to locate successive files that match the file specification used in a call to _dos_findfirst().

_dos_freemem
Syntax: unsigned _dos_freemem(unsigned *segment*);
Include file: <dos.h>
Uses DOS service 0x49 to release memory previously allocated by a call to _dos_allocmem().

_dos_getdate
Syntax: void _dos_getdate(struct dosdate_t *date*);
Include file: <dos.h>
Uses DOS service 0x2A to return the current operating system date.

_dos_getdiskfree
Syntax: unsigned _dos_getdiskfree(unsigned *disk_drive*, struct diskfree_t **diskinfo*);
Include file: <dos.h>
Uses DOS service 0x36 to return disk storage information for the specified disk drive.

_dos_getdrive
Syntax: void _dos_getdrive(unsigned **drive*);
Include file: <dos.h>
Uses DOS service 0x19 to return the current disk drive number (A = 0, B = 1, C = 2, and so on).

_dos_getfileattr
Syntax: unsigned _dos_getfileattr(char **pathname*, unsigned **attribute*);
Include file: <dos.h>
Uses DOS service 0x43 to return the file attributes for specified file.

_dos_getftime
Syntax: unsigned _dos_getftime(int *file_handle*, unsigned **date*, unsigned **time*);
Include file: <dos.h>
Uses DOS service 0x57 to return a file's date-and-time stamp.

_dos_gettime
Syntax: void _dos_gettime(struct dostime_t **time*);
Include file: <dos.h>
Uses DOS service 0x2C to return the current operating system time.

_dos_getvect
Syntax: void(interrupt far **_dos_getvect*(unsigned *interrupt_num*))();
Include file: <dos.h>
Uses DOS service 0x35 to return the interrupt vector for the specified interrupt by *interrupt_num*.

_dos_keep
Syntax: void _dos_keep(unsigned *return_code*, unsigned *num_paragraphs*);
Include file: <dos.h>
Uses DOS service 0x31 to install a memory-resident program.

_dos_open
Syntax: unsigned _dos_open(char **pathname*, unsigned *access_mode*, int **file_handle*);
Include file: <dos.h>
Uses DOS service 0x3D to open the existing file that is specified and return a file handle to the file.

_dos_read
Syntax: int dos_read(int *file_handle*, void far **buffer*,
    unsigned *num_bytes*, unsigned **bytes_read*);
Include file: <dos.h>
Uses DOS service 0x3F to read the number of specified bytes from the file specified by *file_handle* into an input buffer.

_dos_setblock
Syntax: unsigned _dos_setblock(unsigned *new_size*, unsigned
    segment, unsigned **max_mem*);
Include file: <dos.h>
Uses DOS service 0x4A to change the size of a block of memory allocated previously by *_dos_allocmem()*.

_dos_setdate
Syntax: unsigned _dos_setdate(struct dosdate_t **date*);
Include file: <dos.h>
Uses DOS service 0x2B to set the current operating system date.

_dos_setdrive
Syntax: void _dos_setdrive(unsigned int *disk_drive*, unsigned int
    **drives_avail*);
Include file: <dos.h>
Uses DOS service 0x0E to select the current disk drive.

_dos_setfileattr
Syntax: unsigned _dos_setfileattr(char **pathname*, unsigned
    attributes);
Include file: <dos.h>
Uses DOS service 0x43 to set the file attributes for the specified file.

_dos_setftime
Syntax: unsigned _dos_setftime(int *file_handle*, unsigned *date*,
    unsigned *time*);
Include file: <dos.h>
Uses DOS service 0x57 to set a file's date-and-time stamp.

_dos_settime
Syntax: unsigned _dos_settime(struct dostime_t **time*);
Include file: <dos.h>
Uses DOS service 0x2D to set the current operating system time.

_dos_setvect
Syntax: void _dos_setvect(unsigned *interrupt_num*, void (interrupt far
    **handler*)());
Include file: <dos.h>
Uses DOS service 0x25 to assign a new interrupt vector (pointed to by *handler*) to the specified interrupt number.

_dos_write
Syntax: unsigned _dos_write(int *file_handle*, void far *buffer*,
                unsigned *num_bytes*, unsigned **bytes_written*);
Include file: <dos.h>
Uses DOS service 0x40 to write *num_bytes* number of bytes from an output buffer to the specified file.

dup
Syntax: int dup(int *file_handle*);
Include file: <io.h>
Assigns a second file handle to an open file.

dup2
Syntax: int dup2(int *source_handle*, int *target_handle*);
Include file: <io.h>
Copies one file handle to another.

ecvt
Syntax: char *ecvt(double *expression*, int *count*, int **decimal_pos*,
                int **sign*);
Include file: <stdlib.h>
Converts a floating-point expression to a character string *count* characters long. The decimal position and the expression's sign are stored in *decimal_pos* and *sign*, respectively.

_ellipse
Syntax: short far _ellipse(short *fill_flag*, short *x_left*, short *y_top*,
                short *x_right*, short *y_bottom*);
Include file: <graph.h>
Draws an ellipse on the screen in graphics mode, within the coordinates of the specified rectangle.

_enable
Syntax: void _enable(void);
Include file: <dos.h>
Enables 8086 hardware interrupts previously disabled by the _disable() function.

eof
Syntax: int eof(int *file_handle*);
Include file: <io.h>
Returns true (1) if the file associated with the specified file handle has reached the end of the file.

execl

Syntax: int execl(char *pathname*, char *arg0*, char *arg1*, ..., NULL);
Include file: <process.h>
Executes the specified DOS command, using a variable list of command line arguments.

execle

Syntax: int execle(char *pathname*, char *arg0*, ..., NULL, char *envp*[]);
Include file: <process.h>
Executes the specified DOS command (child process), using a variable list of command line arguments and an array of environment entries.

execlp

Syntax: int execlp(char *pathname*, char *arg0*, char *arg1*, ..., NULL);
Include file: <process.h>
Executes the specified DOS command (child process), using a variable list of command line arguments and searching for the command in the directories specified by the PATH environment variable.

execlpe

Syntax: int execlpe(char *pathname*, char *arg0*, ..., NULL, char *envp*[]);
Include file: <process.h>
Executes the specified DOS command (child process), using a variable list of command line arguments and an array of environment entries and searching for the command in the directories specified by the PATH environment variable.

execv

Syntax: int execv(char *pathname*, char *argv*[]);
Include file: <process.h>
Executes the specified DOS command (child process), passing an array of pointers to the command line arguments.

execve

Syntax: int execve(char *pathname*, char *argv*[], char *envp*[]);
Include file: <process.h>
Executes the specified DOS command (child process), passing an array of pointers to the command line and an array of pointers to the environment entries.

execvp

Syntax: int execvp(char *pathname*, char *argv*[]);
Include file: <process.h>
Executes the specified DOS command (child process), passing an array of pointers to the command line arguments and searching for the

command in the directories specified by the PATH environment variable.

execvpe
Syntax: int execvpe(char *pathname*, char *argv*[], char *envp*[]);
Include file: <process.h>
Executes the specified DOS command (child process), passing an array of pointers to the command line and an array of pointers to the environment entries and searching for the command in the directories specified by the PATH environment variable.

exit
Syntax: void exit(int *exit_status*);
Include files: <process.h>, <stdlib.h>
Ends the current program and calls the functions registered by *atexit()* and *onexit()*. Then it returns control to the operating system or to the calling process.

_exit
Syntax: _exit(int *exit_status*);
Include files: <process.h>, <stdlib.h>
Ends the current program and returns control to the operating system or to the calling process.

exp
Syntax: double exp(double *expression*);
Include file: <math.h>
Returns the exponential function of the specified numeric expression.

_expand
Syntax: void *_expand(void *block*, size_t *desired_size*);
Include file: <malloc.h>
Changes the size of a previously allocated block of memory, without moving the block's location within the heap. Returns a void pointer to the allocated memory.

fabs
Syntax: double fabs(double *expression*);
Include file: <math.h>
Returns the absolute value of a floating-point variable.

fclose
Syntax: int fclose(FILE *file_pointer*);
Include file: <stdio.h>
Flushes the buffers associated with the specified file and updates the file's directory entry.

fcloseall
Syntax: int fcloseall(void);
Include file: <stdio.h>
Closes all the open file streams, except stdin, stdout, stderr, stdaux, and stdprn.

fcvt
Syntax: char *fcvt(float *expression*, int *count*, int *decimal_pos*, int *sign*);
Include file: <stdlib.h>
Converts a floating-point expression to a character string *count* characters long. The decimal position and the expression's sign are stored in *decimal_pos* and *sign*, respectively.

fdopen
Syntax: FILE *fdopen(int *file_handle*, char *file_type*);
Include file: <stdio.h>
Associates a stream file pointer with a file that's been opened for low-level file operations by the *open()* or *creat()* function.

feof
Syntax: int feof(FILE *file_pointer*);
Include file: <stdio.h>
Returns true (a nonzero value) if the specified file has reached the end of the file.

ferror
Syntax: int ferror(FILE *file_pointer*);
Include file: <stdio.h>
Returns true (a nonzero value) if the specified file has encountered a reading or writing error.

fflush
Syntax: int fflush(FILE *file_pointer*);
Include file: <stdio.h>
Flushes a buffer's contents to an output file or clears the contents of an input buffer.

_ffree
Syntax: void _ffree(void far *buffer*);
Include file: <malloc.h>
Releases memory from the far heap previously allocated by a call to *_fmalloc()*.

fgetc
Syntax: int fgetc(FILE *stream*);
Include file: <stdio.h>
Reads a character from the specified file, returning the character and incrementing the file pointer to the next character in the file.

fgetchar
Syntax: int fgetchar(void);
Include file: <stdio.h>
Reads and returns a character from stdin.

fgetpos
Syntax: int fgetpos(FILE *file_pointer*, fpos_t *position*);
Include file: <stdio.h>
Returns the file's current position for use by the *fsetpos()* function.

fgets
Syntax: char *fgets(char *string*, int *max_char*, FILE *file_pointer*);
Include file: <stdio.h>
Reads a string of characters from the specified file, advancing the file pointer as appropriate.

fieeetomsbin
Syntax: int fieeetomsbin(float *source*, float *destination*);
Include file: <math.h>
Converts a single-precision floating-point value stored in IEEE format to a floating-point value in Microsoft binary format.

filelength
Syntax: long filelength(int *file_handle*);
Include file: <io.h>
Returns the size in bytes of the file that is associated with the specified file handle.

fileno
Syntax: int fileno(FILE *file_pointer*);
Include file: <stdio.h>
Returns the current file handle that is associated with the specified file pointer.

_floodfill
Syntax: short far _floodfill(short *x_loc*, short *y_loc*, short
            boundary_color);
Include file: <graph.h>
Fills a graphics region on the screen, using the current color and fill mask. It begins filling at the view coordinate point (*x_loc*, *y_loc*).

floor

Syntax: double floor(double *expression*);
Include file: <math.h>
Returns a value of type *double* that is the largest integer smaller than or equal to the specified expression.

flushall

Syntax: int flushall(void);
Include file: <stdio.h>
Flushes to all open output files the file buffers that are associated with them and clears the file buffers that are associated with input file buffers.

_fmalloc

Syntax: void *_fmalloc(size_t *num_bytes*);
Include file: <malloc.h>
Allocates memory dynamically from the far heap.

fmod

Syntax: double fmod(double *numerator*, double *denominator*);
Include file: <math.h>
Returns the floating-point remainder of a double-precision division operation.

fmsbintoieee

Syntax: int fmsbintoieee(float *source*, float *target*);
Include file: <math.h>
Converts a single-precision value in Microsoft binary format to a value in IEEE format.

_fmsize

Syntax: size_t _fmsize(void *ptr*);
Include file: <malloc.h>
Returns the size in bytes of a block of memory dynamically allocated from the far heap by a call to *_fmalloc()*.

fopen

Syntax: FILE *fopen(const char *filename*, const char *access_mode*);
Include file: <stdio.h>
Opens the specified file, returning a file pointer to the file. The *access_mode* parameter specifies how the program will use the file:

"r"	Open file for read access
"w"	Open file for write access
"a"	Open file for append access

(continued)

"r+"	Open file for read/write operations
"w+"	Open file for read/write operations
"a+"	Open file in append mode for read/write operations
"rb"	Open file for read operations in binary mode
"wb"	Open file for write operations in binary mode
"ab"	Open file for append operations in binary mode
"rb+"	Open file for read/write operations in binary mode
"wb+"	Open file for read/write operations in binary mode
"ab+"	Open file in append mode for binary read and write operations

FP_OFF
Syntax: unsigned FP_OFF(void far *address*);
Include file: <dos.h>
Returns the 16-bit offset address portion of a 32-bit far pointer.

_fpreset
Syntax: void _fpreset(void);
Include file: <float.h>
Reinitializes the floating-point math package.

fprintf
Syntax: int fprintf(FILE *file_pointer*, const char *format_specifier*,
        [, *argument*...]);
Include file: <stdio.h>
Writes formatted output to a file.

FP_SEG
Syntax: unsigned FP_SEG(void far *address*);
Include file: <stdio.h>
Returns the 16-bit segment address portion of a 32-bit far pointer.

fputc
Syntax: int fputc(int *character*, FILE *file_pointer*);
Include file: <stdio.h>
Writes a character to the specified file.

fputchar
Syntax: int fputchar(char *character*);
Include file: <stdio.h>
Writes the specified character to stdout.

fputs
Syntax: int fputs(char *string*, FILE *file_pointer*);
Include file: <stdio.h>
Writes a null terminated character string to the specified file, without copying the null character.

fread
Syntax: size_t fread(void *buffer*, size_t *item_size*, size_t *num_items*,
            FILE *file_pointer*);
Include file: <stdio.h>
Reads the specified number of items of size *item_size* from a file and stores them in a buffer.

free
Syntax: void free(void *buffer*);
Include files: <malloc.h>, <stdlib.h>
Releases memory from the heap previously allocated by calls to *calloc()*, *malloc()*, or *realloc()*.

_freect
Syntax: unsigned int _freect(size_t *item_size*);
Include file: <malloc.h>
Returns the number of items of the specified size that can be allocated dynamically from memory.

freopen
Syntax: FILE *freopen(const char *pathname*, const char
            access_mode, FILE *file_pointer*);
Include file: <stdio.h>
Closes the file that is currently associated with a file pointer and opens the second file that is specified by *pathname*, associating it to the file pointer.

frexp
Syntax: double frexp(double *expression*, int *exponent*);
Include file: <math.h>
Breaks apart a floating-point value and returns an exponent and a mantissa.

fscanf
Syntax: int fscanf(FILE *file_pointer*, const char *format_specification*
            [, &*argument*...]);
Include file: <stdio.h>
Reads formatted input from a file into the locations given by the arguments.

fseek
Syntax: int fseek(FILE *file_pointer*, long *offset*, long *start_position*);
Include file: <stdio.h>
Moves the file pointer associated with a specific file to the offset from the specified start position.

fsetpos
Syntax: int fsetpos(FILE *file_pointer*, const fpos_t *position*);
Include file: <stdio.h>
Sets the file pointer position to the location previously stored by the *fgetpos()* function.

fstat
Syntax: int fstat(int *file_handle*, struct stat *fileinfo*);
Include file: <sys\stat.h>
Returns details about the file that is associated with the specified file handle.

ftell
Syntax: long ftell(FILE *file_pointer*);
Include file: <stdio.h>
Returns the file pointer's current offset within the file.

ftime
Syntax: void ftime(struct timeb *time*);
Include file: <sys\timeb.h>
Gets the current time.

fwrite
Syntax: size_t fwrite(const void *buffer*, size_t *item_size*, size_t *num_items*, FILE *file_pointer*);
Include file: <stdio.h>
Writes an output buffer that can contain up to *num_items* items of *item_size* size to the specified file.

gcvt
Syntax: char *gcvt(double *expression*, int *num_digits*, char *buffer*);
Include file: <stdlib.h>
Converts a floating-point expression to a character string and stores the string in the specified buffer. The parameter *num_digits* gives the number of digits that *gcvt()* tries to convert.

_getactivepage
Syntax: short far _getactivepage(void);
Include file: <graph.h>
Returns the current active page number.

_getbkcolor
Syntax: long far _getbkcolor(void);
Include file: <graph.h>
Returns the current graphics background color.

getc
Syntax: int getc(FILE *file_pointer*);
Include file: <stdio.h>
Reads a character from the specified file, advancing the file pointer to point to the next character.

getch
Syntax: int getch(void);
Include file: <conio.h>
Reads a character from the keyboard, without echoing the character to the screen.

getchar
Syntax: int getchar(void);
Include file: <stdio.h>
Reads a character from stdin.

getche
Syntax: int getche(void);
Include file: <conio.h>
Reads a character from the keyboard, echoing to the screen the letter that is associated with the key.

_getcolor
Syntax: short far _getcolor(void);
Include file: <graph.h>
Returns the current graphics pixel color.

_getcurrentposition
Syntax: struct xycoord far _getcurrentposition(void);
Include file: <graph.h>
Returns the view (logical) coordinates of the current graphics position.

getcwd
Syntax: char *getcwd(char *pathname*, int *max_char*);
Include file: <direct.h>
Returns the full pathname of the current directory.

getenv
Syntax: char *getenv(const char *variable_name*);
Include file: <stdlib.h>
Returns the value associated with the environment variable that is specified by *variable_name*.

_getfillmask
Syntax: unsigned char far * far _getfillmask(unsigned char far *mask);
Include file: <graph.h>
Returns the 8-by-8 bit mask (whose bits represent pixels) that is used for graphics fill operations.

_getfontinfo
Syntax: short far _getfontinfo(struct _fontinfo far *fontinfo);
Include file: <graph.h>
Returns in the *fontinfo* structure the current font characteristics.

_getgtextextent
Syntax: short far _getgtextextent(unsigned char far *text);
Include file: <graph.h>
Returns the width in pixels that are needed to print the given character string in the current font using the _outgtext() function.

_getimage
Syntax: void far _getimage(short *x_left*, short *y_top*, short *x_right*, short *y_bottom*, char far *image_buffer*);
Include file: <graph.h>
Stores in the buffer a graphics image that is bounded by the specified rectangle.

_getlinestyle
Syntax: unsigned short far _getlinestyle(void);
Include file: <graph.h>
Returns the bit mask that specifies the graphic's line style, which is used by such functions as _lineto().

_getphyscoord
Syntax: structxycoordfar_getphyscoord(short *x_view*, short *y_view*);
Include file: <graph.h>
Translates view (logical) graphics coordinates into physical device coordinates.

getpid
Syntax: int getpid(void);
Include file: <process.h>
Returns the unique process ID (PID) of the current process.

_getpixel
Syntax: short far _getpixel(short *x_loc*, short *y_loc*);
Include file: <graph.h>
Returns the pixel value at the specified graphics coordinates.

gets
Syntax: char *gets(char *string*);
Include file: <stdio.h>
Reads a line of input from stdin and stores it in the specified buffer.

_gettextcolor
Syntax: short far *_gettextcolor(void);
Include file: <graph.h>
Returns the current text color used by the _outtext() function.

_gettextcursor
Syntax: short far _gettextcursor(void);
Include file: <graph.h>
Returns the shape of the cursor in a text video mode.

_gettextposition
Syntax: struct rccoord far _gettextposition(void);
Include file: <graph.h>
Returns the current row and column position used for text output by the _outtext() function.

_getvideoconfig
Syntax: struct videoconfig far * far _getvideoconfig(struct
                                    videoconfig far *configuration);
Include file: <graph.h>
Returns the current video environment. The include file graph.h defines the *videoconfig* structure.

_getviewcoord
Syntax: struct xycoord far _getviewcoord(short *x_physical*, short
                                    y_physical);
Include file: <graph.h>
Translates physical device coordinates into view (logical) coordinates.

_getvisualpage
Syntax: short far _getvisualpage(void);
Include file: <graph.h>
Returns the current visual page number.

getw
Syntax: int getw(FILE *file_pointer*);
Include file: <stdio.h>
Returns a binary value that is of type *int* from a file and advances the file pointer to the next position.

_getwindowcoord
Syntax: struct _wxycoord far _getwindowcoord(short *x*, short *y*)
Include file: <graph.h>
Translates view coordinates to window coordinates.

gmtime
Syntax: struct tm *gmtime(const time_t **time*);
Include file: <time.h>
Returns the current Greenwich mean time.

halloc
Syntax: void huge *halloc(long *num_elements*, size_t *element_size*);
Include file: <malloc.h>
Allocates memory for a huge array.

_harderr
Syntax: harderr_harderr(void(far *handler*)());
Include file: <dos.h>
Installs a user-defined function that serves as an INT 0x24 critical error handler.

_hardresume
Syntax: void _hardresume(int *status*);
Include file: <dos.h>
Returns control to DOS from a user-defined critical error handler installed by the _harderr() function.

_hardretn
Syntax: void _hardretn(int *error*);
Include file: <dos.h>
Returns control from a user-defined critical error handler installed by the _harderr() function to the program that's causing the error.

_heapchk, _fheapchk, _nheapchk
Syntax: int _heapchk(void);
Syntax: int _fheapchk(void);
Syntax: int _nheapchk(void);
Include file: <malloc.h>
Returns heap status information. If you are working with the compact, large, or huge memory model, _heapchk() is defined as _fheapchk() to check the far heap. For small and medium memory models, _heapchk() is defined as _nheapchk() to check the near heap. This function returns one of the constants on the following page.

_HEAPBADBEGIN   Initial header information is bad.
_HEAPBADNODE   A node in the heap is damaged.
_HEAPEMPTY   Heap has not been initialized.
_HEAPOK   Heap is consistent.

_heapset, _fheapset, _nheapset

Syntax: int _heapset(unsigned *heap_value*);
Syntax: int _fheapset(unsigned *heap_value*);
Syntax: int _nheapset(unsigned *heap_value*);
Include file: <malloc.h>

Initializes the free entries in the heap to the specified value and also performs a heap consistency check. If you are working with the compact, large, or huge memory model, *_heapset()* is defined as *_fheapset()* to initialize the far heap. For small and medium memory models, *_heapset()* is defined as *_nheapset()* to initialize the near heap.

_heapwalk, _fheapwalk, _nheapwalk

Syntax: int _heapwalk(struct _heapinfo *heap_entry*);
Syntax: int _fheapwalk(struct _heapinfo *heap_entry*);
Syntax: int _nheapwalk(struct _heapinfo *heap_entry*);
Include file: <malloc.h>

Traverses the heap's nodes and returns status information. If you are working with the compact, large, or huge memory model, *_heapwalk()* is defined as *_fheapwalk()* to traverse the far heap. For small and medium memory models, *_heapwalk()* is defined as *_nheapwalk()* to traverse the near heap. The *_heapwalk()* function traverses the heap one node at a time, returning information about the node in the *_heapinfo* structure:

```
struct _heapinfo
    {
    int far *_pentry; /* entry pointer */
    size_t_size;      /* size in bytes */
    int _useflag;
    };
```

This function also returns one of the following constants that give status information:

_HEAPBADBEGIN   Initial header information is bad.
_HEAPBADNODE   A node in the heap is damaged.
_HEAPEMPTY   Heap has not been initialized.

(continued)

_HEAPBADPTR   A valid pointer to the heap was not used in the *heap_entry* parameter.

_HEAPOK   Heap is consistent.

_HEAPEND   End of heap has been reached.

hfree
Syntax: void hfree(void huge *array*);
Include file: <malloc.h>
Releases memory that was allocated for a huge array by the *halloc()* function.

hypot
Syntax: double hypot(double *x*, double *y*);
Include file: <math.h>
Returns the length of a right triangle's hypotenuse. The triangle's two sides are given by *x* and *y*.

_imagesize
Syntax: long far _imagesize(short *x_left*, short *y_top*, short *x_right*, short *y_bottom*);
Include file: <graph.h>
Returns the number of bytes needed to store an image that is bounded by the specified rectangle.

inp
Syntax: int inp(unsigned *port*);
Include file: <conio.h>
Reads a byte value from the specified input port.

inpw
Syntax: int inpw(unsigned *port*)
Include file: <conio.h>
Reads a 16-bit (word) value from the specified input port.

int86
Syntax: int int86(int *interrupt_number*, union REGS **inregs*, union REGS **outregs*);
Include files: <bios.h>, <dos.h>
Executes the specified 8086 interrupt, passing the register arguments in the *inregs* union. The resulting register values are copied to the *outregs* union.

int86x
Syntax: int int86x(int *interrupt_number*, union REGS **inregs*, union REGS **outregs*, struct SREGS **segregs*);
Include files: <bios.h>, <dos.h>

Executes the specified 8086 service, passing the register arguments in the *inregs* union. This function also supports the segment registers ES, CS, SS, and DS so that it is possible to specify which segment or pointer should be used in the function call. The resulting register values are copied to the *outregs* union.

intdos
Syntax: int intdos(union REGS *inregs*, union REGS *outregs*);
Include file: <dos.h>
Uses int 0x21 to execute a DOS system service, passing the register arguments in the *inregs* union.

intdosx
Syntax: int intdosx(union REGS *inregs*, union REGS *outregs*, struct SREGS *segregs*);
Include file: <dos.h>
Uses int 0x21 to execute a DOS system service, passing the register arguments in the *inregs* union. This function also supports the segment registers ES, CS, DS, and SS, so that it is possible to specify which segment or pointer should be used in the function call. The resulting register values are copied to the *outregs* union.

isalnum
Syntax: int isalnum(int *character*);
Include file: <ctype.h>
Returns a value of 1 if the specified character is in the range 'A' through 'Z', 'a' through 'z', or '0' through '9'.

isalpha
Syntax: int isalpha(int *character*);
Include file: <ctype.h>
Returns a value of 1 if the specified character is in the range 'A' through 'Z' or 'a' through 'z'.

isascii
Syntax: int isascii(int *character*);
Include file: <ctype.h>
Returns a value of 1 if the specified character is an ASCII character in the range 0 through 127.

isatty
Syntax: int isatty(int *file_handle*);
Include file: <io.h>
Returns a value of 1 if the specified handle is associated with a device (terminal, console, printer, or serial port) or a value of 0 if the handle is associated with a file.

iscntrl
Syntax: int iscntrl(int *character*);
Include file: <conio.h>
Returns a value of 1 if the specified character is a control character in the range 0 through 31 or is 127.

isdigit
Syntax: int isdigit(int *character*);
Include file: <ctype.h>
Returns a value of 1 if the specified character is a digit in the range '0' through '9'.

isgraph
Syntax: int isgraph(int *character*);
Include file: <ctype.h>
Returns a value of 1 if the specified character is a printable character in the range 33 through 126, excluding the space character.

islower
Syntax: int islower(int *character*);
Include file: <ctype.h>
Returns a value of 1 if the specified character is lowercase in the range 'a' through 'z'.

isprint
Syntax: int isprint(int *character*);
Include file: <ctype.h>
Returns a value of 1 if the specified character is a printable character in the range 32 through 126.

ispunct
Syntax: int ispunct(int *character*);
Include file: <ctype.h>
Returns a value of 1 if the specified character is a punctuation character such as a comma, a semicolon, or a period.

isspace
Syntax: int isspace(int *character*);
Include file: <ctype.h>
Returns a value of 1 if the specified character is a whitespace character (tab, linefeed, vertical tab, formfeed, carriage return, or space).

isupper
Syntax: int isupper(char *character*);
Include file: <ctype.h>
Returns a value of 1 if the specified character is uppercase in the range 'A' through 'Z'.

isxdigit

Syntax: int isxdigit(int *character*);
Include file: <ctype.h>
Returns a value of 1 if the specified character is a hexadecimal digit in the range 'A' through 'F', 'a' through 'f', or '0' through '9'.

itoa

Syntax: char *itoa(int *value*, char *ascii*, int *radix*);
Include file: <stdlib.h>
Converts an integer value to its character string representation, using the specified radix (base).

kbhit

Syntax: int kbhit(void);
Include file: <conio.h>
Returns a value of 1 if a character is present in the keyboard buffer.

labs

Syntax: long labs(long *expression*);
Include files: <math.h>, <stdlib.h>
Returns the absolute value of a long-integer expression.

ldexp

Syntax: double ldexp(double *x*, int *exponent*);
Include file: <math.h>
Returns *x* times the value of 2 to the specified exponent.

ldiv

Syntax: struct ldiv_t ldiv(long int *numerator*, long int *denominator*);
Include file: <stdlib.h>
Returns the quotient and remainder for a long-integer division.

lfind

Syntax: char *lfind(char *key_value*, char *base_address*, unsigned *num_elements*, unsigned *element_width*, int(*comp*) (const void *a*, const void *b*));
Include file: <search.h>
Searches an array for a specific value. The program must define the *comp()* function, which uses pointers to compare two values.

_lineto

Syntax: short far _lineto(short *x_loc*, short *y_loc*);
Include file: <graph.h>
Draws a line from the current graphics position to the specified view (logical) coordinate.

localtime
Syntax: struct tm *localtime(consttime_t *time);
Include file: <time.h>
Returns a structure that contains the current local time, taking into account the time zone and daylight saving time.

locking
Syntax: int locking(int file_handle, int lock_mode, long num_bytes);
Include file: <io.h>
Locks the number of specified bytes in a file, beginning from the current file positions. Locking is useful in a file-sharing environment because locking the bytes prevents other processes from reading or writing them.

log
Syntax: double log(double expression);
Include file: <math.h>
Returns the natural logarithm of the specified expression.

log10
Syntax: double log10(double expression);
Include file: <math.h>
Returns the base 10 logarithm of the specified expression.

longjmp
Syntax: void longjmp(jmp_buf environment, int return_value);
Include file: <setjmp.h>
Performs a nonlocal *goto* by restoring the register environment (stored in the *environment* parameter) previously saved by the *setjmp()* function.

_lrotl
Syntax: unsigned long _lrotl(unsigned long value, int num_shifts);
Include file: <stdlib.h>
Rotates the bits of an unsigned long-integer value to the left by the number of bits specified by *num_shifts*.

_lrotr
Syntax: unsigned _lrotr(unsigned long value, int num_shifts);
Include file: <stdlib.h>
Rotates the bits of an unsigned long-integer value to the right by the number of bits specified by *num_shifts*.

lsearch

Syntax: char *lsearch(char *key_value, char *base, unsigned num_elements, unsigned element_width, int(*comp) (void *a, void *b));
Include file: <search.h>
Searches an array for a specific value. The program must define the comp() function, which uses pointers to compare two values. If the value isn't found, lsearch() adds it to the end of the array.

lseek

Syntax: long lseek(int file_handle, long num_bytes, int start_position);
Include file: <io.h>
Moves the file pointer associated with a file handle by the specified number of bytes and from the specified starting location:

SEEK_CUR	Seeks from current location
SEEK_END	Seeks from end of file
SEEK_SET	Seeks from start of file

ltoa

Syntax: char *ltoa(long int value, char *ascii, int radix);
Include file: <stdlib.h>
Converts a long-integer value to its character string representation, using the specified radix (base).

_makepath

Syntax: void _makepath(char *pathname, char *drive, char *directory, char *filename, char *extension);
Include file: <stdlib.h>
Builds a complete pathname, returned in pathname, from a drive letter, directory, filename, and extension.

malloc

Syntax: void *malloc(size_t num_bytes);
Include files: <malloc.h>, <stdlib.h>
Allocates memory dynamically from the heap. If you work with the compact, large, or huge memory model, malloc() is mapped to _fmalloc(). Similarly, for small and medium memory models, malloc() is mapped to _nmalloc().

matherr

Syntax: int matherr(struct exception *exception_info);
Include file: <math.h>
Provides a user-defined exception handler for errors generated by the run-time library math routines.

max
Syntax: max(*x*, *y*)
Include file: <stdlib.h>
Returns the larger of two values.

_memavl
Syntax: size_t _memavl(void);
Include file: <malloc.h>
Returns the amount of heap space available for dynamic memory allocation.

memccpy
Syntax: void *memccpy(void **target*, void **source*, int *character*, unsigned *num_bytes*);
Include files: <memory.h>, <string.h>
Copies from one location to another either the bytes that precede the first occurrence of the specified character or the specified number of bytes if the character was not found with that number of bytes.

memchr
Syntax: void *memchr(void **buffer*, int *character*, size_t *num_bytes*);
Include files: <memory.h>, <string.h>
Searches for the first occurrence of the specified character in the first *num_bytes* bytes of a memory buffer. If successful, *memchr()* returns a pointer to the character.

memcmp
Syntax: int memcmp(const void **buffer1*, const void **buffer2*, size_t *num_bytes*);
Include files: <memory.h>, <string.h>
Compares the first *num_bytes* bytes of two memory buffers.

memcpy
Syntax: void *memcpy(void **target*, void **source*, size_t *num_bytes*);
Include files: <memory.h>, <string.h>
Copies the specified number of bytes from a source buffer to a destination buffer.

memicmp
Syntax: int memicmp(void **buffer1*, void **buffer2*, unsigned *num_bytes*);
Include files: <memory.h>, <string.h>
Compares the first *num_bytes* bytes of two memory buffers, ignoring case difference in the letters that are compared.

_memmax
Syntax: size_t _memmax(void);
Include file: <malloc.h>
Returns the size of the largest contiguous block available for allocation from the near heap.

memmove
Syntax: void *memmove(void *target*, const void *source*, size_t num_bytes*);
Include file: <string.h>
Copies the specified number of characters from the source to target memory buffers.

memset
Syntax: void *memset(void *target*, int *character*, size_t *num_bytes*);
Include files: <memory.h>, <string.h>
Sets the first *num_bytes* bytes of a memory buffer to the specified character.

min
Syntax: min(*x*, *y*);
Include file: <stdlib.h>
Returns the smaller of two values.

mkdir
Syntax: int mkdir(char *pathname*);
Include file: <direct.h>
Creates the specified subdirectory.

mktemp
Syntax: char *mktemp(char *template*);
Include file: <io.h>
Returns a unique filename, based upon the specified template.

mktime
Syntax: time_t mktime(struct tm *time*);
Include file: <time.h>
Converts a local time to a calendar time.

modf
Syntax: double modf(double *expression*, double *intpart*);
Include file: <math.h>
Breaks a floating-point value into its integer and fractional components. The function returns the fractional component, and *intpart* stores the integer component.

movedata
Syntax: void movedata(unsigned *source_segment*, unsigned *source_offset*, unsigned *target_segment*, unsigned *target_offset*, unsigned *num_bytes*);
Include files: <memory.h>, <string.h>
Copies the specified number of bytes from one segment and the offset address combination to another.

_moveto
Syntax: struct xycoord far _moveto(short xcoord, short ycoord);
Include file: <graph.h>
Moves the graphic's current position to the specified coordinates.

_msize
Syntax: size_t _msize(void *ptr*);
Include file: <malloc.h>
Returns the size of a block of dynamically allocated memory in bytes. If you work with the compact, large, or huge memory model, *_msize()* is mapped to *_fmsize()*. Similarly, *_msize()* is mapped to *_nmsize()* for small and medium models.

_nfree
Syntax: void _nfree(void near *buffer*)
Include file: <malloc.h>
Releases from the near heap memory that was previously allocated by a call to *_malloc()*.

_nmalloc
Syntax: void far *_nmalloc(size_t *num_bytes*);
Include file: <malloc.h>
Allocates memory dynamically from the near heap.

_nmsize
Syntax: size_t _nmsize(void *ptr*);
Include file: <malloc.h>
Returns the size (in bytes) of a block of memory that was dynamically allocated from the near heap by a call to *_nmalloc()*.

onexit
Syntax: onexit_t onexit(onexit_t *function*);
Include file: <stdlib.h>
Adds a function to the list of functions that C executes when the program completes its execution. The *onexit()* function processes in exactly the same way as the *atexit()* run-time library routine. Because *atexit()* is part of the ANSI standard, you should use *atexit()* in place of *onexit()*.

open
Syntax: int open(char *pathname*, int *mode* [, int *create_mode*]);
Include file: <io.h>
Opens a file as specified, returning a file handle for use in future file input/output operations.

_outgtext
Syntax: void far _outgtext(unsigned char far *text*)
Include file: <graph.h>
Writes the specified text to the screen at the current graphics position.

outp
Syntax: int outp(unsigned *port*, int *value*);
Include file: <conio.h>
Outputs a byte value to the specified port address.

outpw
Syntax: int outpw(unsigned *port*, unsigned *value*);
Include file: <conio.h>
Outputs a 16-bit (word) value to the specified port address.

_outtext
Syntax: void far _outtext(unsigned char far *text*);
Include file: <graph.h>
At the current cursor position, writes the specified text to the current video page and text window.

perror
Syntax: void perror(const char *message*);
Include files: <stdio.h>, <stdlib.h>
Displays a program-defined error message to stderr, followed by the system error message for the last library call that failed.

_pg_analyzechart
Syntax: short far _pg_analyzechart(chartenv far *chart_environment*,
　　　　　　　char * far *category_names*, float far *values*, short
　　　　　　　number_of_values);
Include file: <pgchart.h>
Analyzes a column, bar, or line chart for a series of data values, without displaying the image. This support function is used primarily by presentation graphics functions.

_pg_analyzechartms
Syntax: short far _pg_analyzechartms(chartenv far
　　　　　　　chart_environment, char * far *category_names*,
　　　　　　　float far *values*, short *number_of_series*, short
　　　　　　　number_of_values, short *array_dimension*, char * far
　　　　　　　series_labels);

Include file: <pgchart.h>
Analyzes multiple column, bar, or line charts for a series of data values, without displaying the image. This support function is used primarily by presentation graphics functions.

_pg_analyzepie
Syntax: short far _pg_analyzepie(chartenv far *chart_environment, char * far *category_names, float far *values, short far *explode_flag, short number_of_values);

Include file: <pgchart.h>
Analyzes a pie chart for a series of data values, without displaying the image. This support function is used primarily by presentation graphics functions.

_pg_analyzescatter
Syntax: short far _pg_analyzescatter(chartenv far *chart_environment, float far *x_values, float far *y_values, short number_of_values);

Include file: <pgchart.h>
Analyzes a scatter chart for a series of x and y data values, without displaying the image. This support function is used primarily by presentation graphics functions.

_pg_analyzescatterms
Syntax: short far _pg_analyzescatterms(chartenv far *chart_environment, float far *x_values, float far *y_values, short number_of_series, short number_of_values, short array_dimension, char * far *series_labels);

Include file: <pgchart.h>
Analyzes a scatter chart for a multiple series of x and y data values, without displaying the image. This support function is used primarily by presentation graphics functions.

_pg_chart
Syntax: short far _pg_chart(chartenv far *chart_environment, char * far *category_names, float far *values, short number_of_values);

Include file: <pgchart.h>
Generates a column, bar, or line chart for a series of data values.

_pg_chartms
Syntax: short far _pg_chartms(chartenv far *chart_environment, char * far *category_names, float far *values, short number_of_series, short number_of_values, short array_dimension, char * far *series_labels);

Include file: <pgchart.h>

Generates multiple column, bar, or line charts for a series of data values. Each series must have the same number of values.

_pg_chartpie
Syntax: short far _pg_chartpie(chartenv far *chart_environment*, char * far *category_names*, float far *values*, short far *explode_flag*, short *number_of_values*);
Include file: <pgchart.h>
Generates a pie chart for a series of data values.

_pg_chartscatter
Syntax: short far _pg_chartscatter(chartenv far *chart_environment*, float far *x_values*, float far *y_values*, short *number_of_values*);
Include file: <pgchart.h>
Generates a scatter chart for a series of x and y data values.

_pg_chartscatterms
Syntax: short far _pg_chartscatterms(chartenv far *chart_environment*, float far *x_values*, float far *y_values*, short *number_of_series*, short *number_of_values*, short *array_dimension*, char * far *series_labels*);
Include file: <pgchart.h>
Generates a scatter chart for multiple series of x and y data values.

_pg_defaultchart
Syntax: short far _pg_defaultchart(chartenv far *chart_environment*, short *chart_type*, short *chart_style*);
Include file: <pgchart.h>
Initializes the chart environment to reflect the specified chart type and style. The chart can be any of five chart types: bar, column, line, scatter, or pie.

_pg_getchardef
Syntax: void far _pg_getchardef(short *char_number*, charmap far *char_definition*);
Include file: <pgchart.h>
Returns the 8-by-8 pixel bit map of the character with the ASCII value of *char_number*. The bit map is stored in *char_definition*. This support function is used primarily by presentation graphics functions.

_pg_getpalette
Syntax: short far _pg_getpalette(paletteentry far *array_of_palettes*);
Include file: <pgchart.h>
Retrieves the palette colors, line styles, fill patterns, and plot characters for all palettes. This support function is used primarily by presentation graphics functions.

_pg_getstyleset
Syntax: void far _pg_getstyleset(short far *styleset*);
Include file: <pgchart.h>
Retrieves the contents of the current styleset. This support function is used primarily by presentation graphics functions.

_pg_hlabelchart
Syntax: short far _pg_hlabelchart(chartenv far *chart_environment*,
            short *x_start*, short *y_start*, short *color*, char far
            **label*);
Include file: <pgchart.h>
Writes text on a chart horizontally, beginning at the point (*x_start*, *y_start*). This support function is used primarily by presentation graphics functions.

_pg_initchart
Syntax: short far _pg_initchart(void)
Include file: <pgchart.h>
Initializes the presentation graphics package. This function must be used in a program before any other function from the pgchart.h include file is called.

_pg_resetpalette
Syntax: short far _pg_resetpalette(void);
Include file: <pgchart.h>
Resets the palette colors, line styles, fill patterns, and plot characters to their default values. This support function is used primarily by presentation graphics functions.

_pg_resetstyleset
Syntax: void far _pg_resetstyleset(void);
Include file: <pgchart.h>
Resets the styleset to its default values. This support function is used primarily by presentation graphics functions.

_pg_setchardef
Syntax: void far _pg_setchardef(short *char_number*, charmap far
            **char_definition*);
Include file: <pgchart.h>
Sets the 8-by-8 pixel bit map for the character with the ASCII value of *char_number* to the bit map that is stored in *char_definition*. This support function is used primarily by presentation graphics functions.

_pg_setpalette
Syntax: short far _pg_setpalette(paletteentry far *array_of_palettes*);
Include file: <pgchart.h>

Sets the palette colors, line styles, fill patterns, and plot characters for all palettes. This support function is used primarily by presentation graphics functions.

_pg_setstyleset
Syntax: void far _pg_setstyleset(short far *styleset*);
Include file: <pgchart.h>
Sets the contents of the current styleset. This support function is used primarily by presentation graphics functions.

_pg_vlabelchart
Syntax: short far _pg_vlabelchart(chartenv far *chart_environment*,
short *x_start*, short *y_start*, short *color*, char far *label*);
Include file: <pgchart.h>
Writes text on a chart vertically, beginning at the point (x_start, y_start). This support function is used primarily by presentation graphics functions.

_pie
Syntax: short far _pie(short *fill_flag*, short *x_left*, short *y_top*, short *x_right*, short *y_bottom*, short *x_start*, short *y_start*, short *x_stop*, short *y_stop*);
Include file: <graph.h>
Draws a pie-shaped wedge in graphics mode. The pie's center is the center of the rectangle that is defined by the points (x_left, y_top) and (x_right, y_bottom). The pie's arc is drawn clockwise, beginning at the point (x_start, y_start) and ending at (x_stop, y_stop). Lines connect the center and the two endpoints to complete the pie shape.

pow
Syntax: double pow(double *expression*, double *power*);
Include file: <math.h>
Returns the value of the expression raised to the specified power.

printf
Syntax: int printf(const char *format_specification*[, *argument*...]);
Include file: <stdio.h>
Writes formatted output to stdout.

putc
Syntax: int putc(int *character*, FILE *file_pointer*);
Include file: <stdio.h>
Writes *character* to the specified file.

putch
Syntax: int putch(int *character*);
Include file: <conio.h>
Writes the specified character directly to the console, as opposed to writing to stdout.

putchar
Syntax: int putchar(int *character*);
Include file: <stdio.h>
Writes the specified character to stdout.

putenv
Syntax: int putenv(char **environment_entry*);
Include file: <stdlib.h>
Adds or changes an entry in the DOS environment table.

_putimage
Syntax: void far _putimage(short *x_loc*, short *y_loc*, char far
          *image_buffer, short *display_flag*);
Include file: <graph.h>
Displays a graphics image previously saved to a buffer by the *_getimage()* function.

puts
Syntax: int puts(const char **string*);
Include file: <stdio.h>
Writes a NULL terminated character string to stdout. When the *puts()* function encounters the NULL character ('\0'), it writes a newline character ('\n').

putw
Syntax: int putw(int *value*, FILE **file_pointer*);
Include file: <stdio.h>
Writes a binary value that is of type *int* to the specified file.

qsort
Syntax: void qsort(void **base_address*, size_t *num_elements*,
          size_t *element_width*, int(**compare*)(const void **a*, const
          void **b*));
Include files: <stdlib.h>, <search.h>
Sorts an array of values, using the quick-sort algorithm. The program must define the *compare()* function that uses pointers to compare two values.

raise
Syntax: int raise(int *signal*);
Include file: <signal.h>
Raises a signal. The *raise()* function is often used to test exception handling routines installed by the *signal()* function.

rand
Syntax: int rand(void);
Include file: <stdlib.h>
Returns a pseudo-random number, in the range 0 through 32,767.

read
Syntax: int read(int *file_handle*, char **buffer*, unsigned *num_bytes*);
Include file: <io.h>
Reads into a buffer *num_bytes* of data from the file that is associated with the specified file handle.

realloc
Syntax: void *realloc(void *ptr*, size_t *desired_size*);
Include files: <malloc.h>, <stdlib.h>
Changes the size of a previously allocated block of memory.

_rectangle
Syntax: short far _rectangle(short *fill_flag*, short *x_left*, short *y_top*, short *x_right*, short *y_bottom*);
Include file: <graph.h>
Draws a rectangle on the screen, using the specified coordinate.

_registerfonts
Syntax: short far _registerfonts(unsigned char far **filename*);
Include file: <graph.h>
Initializes the fonts graphics system. This function must be called before any other font-related function can be used.

_remapallpalette
Syntax: short far _remapallpalette(long far **colors*);
Include file: <graph.h>
Changes the colors associated with the graphics palette.

_remappalette
Syntax: long far _remappalette(short *pixelcolor*, long *color*);
Include file: <graph.h>
Reassigns the color value *pixelcolor* in the current palette to *color*.

remove
Syntax: int remove(const char **pathname*);
Include files: <io.h>, <stdio.h>
Deletes the specified file from the disk.

rename
Syntax: int rename(const char *oldname*, const char *newname*);
Include files: <io.h>, <stdio.h>
Renames an existing file.

rewind
Syntax: void rewind(FILE *file_pointer*);
Include file: <stdio.h>
Resets a file pointer back to the start of the file.

rmdir
Syntax: int rmdir(char *pathname*);
Include file: <direct.h>
Removes the specified directory. The *pathname* parameter must specify a subdirectory that is not the current working directory and does not contain any file.

rmtmp
Syntax: int rmtmp(void);
Include file: <stdio.h>
Removes all temporary files in the current directory that were created by the *tmpfile()* function.

_rotl
Syntax: unsigned _rotl(unsigned int *value*, int *num_shifts*);
Include file: <stdlib.h>
Rotates the bits of an unsigned integer to the left, by the number of bits specified by *num_shifts*.

_rotr
Syntax: unsigned _rotr(unsigned int *value*, int *num_shifts*);
Include file: <stdlib.h>
Rotates the bits of an unsigned integer to the right, by the number of bits specified by *num_shifts*.

sbrk
Syntax: void *sbrk(int *increment*);
Include file: <malloc.h>
Changes the location of a program's break value, which is the address of the first value beyond the heap. The *sbrk()* function adds *increment* bytes to the address, adding (or subtracting if *increment* is negative) to the amount of memory allocated from the heap.

scanf
Syntax: int scanf(const char *format_specifications*[, &*argument*...]);
Include file: <stdio.h>
Reads formatted input from stdin into the locations given by the arguments.

_searchenv

Syntax: void _searchenv(char *filename, char *environment_entry,
            char *pathname);
Include file: <stdlib.h>
Searches for filename in the directory path that is associated with the specified environment entry. If the file is found, _searchenv() copies the path into pathname.

segread

Syntax: void segread(struct SREGS *segment_registers);
Include file: <dos.h>
Places the current values of the segment registers CS, DS, SS, and ES in a structure of type SREGS.

_selectpalette

Syntax: short far _selectpalette(short palette_number);
Include file: <graph.h>
Selects a background and a set of three colors for use in _MRES4COLOR or _MRESNOCOLOR video mode.

_setactivepage

Syntax: short far _setactivepage(short video_page);
Include file: <graph.h>
Selects the video display page (that is in memory) to which graphics output or text from the _outtext() function is written.

_setbkcolor

Syntax: long far _setbkcolor(long color);
Include file: <graph.h>
Sets the current graphics background color to the specified pixel color.

setbuf

Syntax: void setbuf(FILE *file_pointer, char *buffer);
Include file: <stdio.h>
Allows a program to specify the buffer to be used for disk input/output operations that are performed on the file to which file_pointer points.

_setcliprgn

Syntax: void far _setcliprgn(short x_left, short y_top, short x_right,
            short y_bottom);
Include file: <graph.h>
Defines the coordinates of the graphics clip region. Graphics and text displayed after a call to _setcliprgn() will be visible only in the rectangle defined by the points (x_left, y_top) and (x_right, y_bottom).

_setcolor
Syntax: short far _setcolor(short *color*);
Include file: <graph.h>
Sets the current graphics foreground color.

_setfillmask
Syntax: void far _setfillmask(unsigned char far *fillmask*);
Include file: <graph.h>
Defines the fill mask (an 8-by-8 array of bits) used for graphics operations.

_setfont
Syntax: short far _setfont(unsigned char far *options*)
Include file: <graph.h>
Sets the current font to the single font that has the characteristics that are specified in the *options* string

setjmp
Syntax: int setjmp(jmp_buf *environment_state*);
Include file: <setjmp.h>
Saves the current contents of the stack so that the *longjmp()* function can use the contents later to reset the stack, performing nonlocal branching.

_setlinestyle
Syntax: void far _setlinestyle(unsigned short *line_style*);
Include file: <graph.h>
Specifies the style or pattern of the lines used in graphics operations.

setmode
Syntax: int setmode(int *file_handle*, int *mode*);
Include file: <io.h>
Sets a file's translation mode to binary or text.

_setpixel
Syntax: short far _setpixel(short *x*, short *y*);
Include file: <graph.h>
Turns on the pixel at the point specified by *x* and *y*.

_settextcolor
Syntax: short far _settextcolor(short *color*);
Include file: <graph.h>
Sets the color value used by the _outtext() function for text output:

0 Black	4 Red	8 Dark gray	12 Light red
1 Blue	5 Magenta	9 Light blue	13 Light magenta
2 Green	6 Brown	10 Light green	14 Yellow
3 Cyan	7 White	11 Light cyan	15 Bright white

_settextcursor
Syntax: short far _settextcursor(short *attribute*);
Include file: <graph.h>
Sets the cursor shape to the one specified by *attribute*. The cursor can be an underline, a full block, a double underline, or invisible.

_settextposition
Syntax: struct rccoord far _settextposition(short *row*, short *column*);
Include file: <graph.h>
Sets the row and column position for text output via functions such as *_outtext()* and *printf()*.

_settextrows
Syntax: short far _settextrows(short *rows*);
Include file: <graph.h>
Sets the number of text rows used in text modes. This function can be used only with hardware that supports 43-line or 50-line modes.

_settextwindow
Syntax: void far _settextwindow(short *x_left*, short *y_top*, short *x_right*, short *y_bottom*);
Include file: <graph.h>
Specifies the coordinates of the window used for text output.

setvbuf
Syntax: int setvbuf(FILE **file_pointer*, char **buffer*, int *buffer_type*, size_t *buffer_size*);
Include file: <stdio.h>
Allows the program to specify both the buffer that it uses for file I/O performed on the file that *file_pointer* points to and the buffering technique:

_IOFBF	Full buffering
_IOLBF	Full buffering (same as _IOFBF)
_IONBF	No buffering

_setvideomode
Syntax: short far _setvideomode(short *video_mode*);
Include file: <graph.h>
Selects the current video display mode.

_setvideomoderows
Syntax: short far _setvideomoderows(short *mode*, short *rows*);
Include file: <graph.h>
Selects the current video display mode and sets the number of text rows used in a text mode.

_setvieworg
Syntax: struct xycoord far _setvieworg(short *x*, short *y*);
Include file: <graph.h>
Places the origin (0,0) of the view (logical) coordinates used by the graphics routines at the specified physical device coordinate.

_setviewport
Syntax: void far _setviewport(short *x_left*, short *y_top*, short *x_right*, short *y_bottom*);
Include file: <graph.h>
Defines a clipping region on the graphics screen and then assigns the origin of the view (logical) coordinates to the upper-left corner.

_setvisualpage
Syntax: short far _setvisualpage(short *video_page*);
Include file: <graph.h>
Selects the video display page that is visible on your screen.

_setwindow
Syntax: short far _setwindow(short *invert_flag*, double *win_x1*, double *win_y1*, double *win_x2*, double *win_y2*);
Include file: <graph.h>
Defines the graphics window as the rectangle specified by the points (*win_x1*, *win_y1*) and (*win_x2*, *win_y2*).

signal
Syntax: void (**signal*(int *event*, void *(*function*)(int *event* [,int *subcode*])))(int *event*);
Include file: <signal.h>
Specifies a program-defined function to serve as an interrupt handler for the signal indicated in the *signal* parameter, which can be one of the following values:

SIGABRT	Program termination with an exit status of 3
SIGFPE	Floating-point error
SIGILL	Illegal instruction
SIGINT	Ctrl+C interrupt 0x23
SIGSEGV	Illegal storage access
SIGTERM	Program termination request

sin
Syntax: double sin(double *expression*);
Include file: <math.h>
Returns the sine of a numeric expression.

sinh

Syntax: double sinh(double *expression*)
Include file: <math.h>
Returns the hyperbolic sine of a numeric expression.

sopen

Syntax: int sopen(char *pathname*, int *mode*, int *share_access* [,int
  permission]);
Include file: <io.h>
Opens a file for shared read and write operations.

spawnl

Syntax: int spawnl(int *invoke_flag*, char *pathname*, char *arg0*, char
  arg1, ..., NULL);
Include file: <process.h>
Executes the specified DOS command (child process), using a NULL terminated list of arguments. When the command completes, the program resumes control. The following flags dictate how DOS loads the program:

P_WAIT	Suspends parent program execution until spawned program completes
P_NOWAIT	Continues to execute parent process concurrently with spawned program
P_OVERLAY	Overlays parent process in memory with spawned program; same effect as using *execl()* function

spawnle

Syntax: int spawnle(int *invoke_flag*, char *pathname*, char *arg0*, char
  arg1, ..., NULL, char *envp*[]);
Include file: <process.h>
Executes the specified DOS command (child process), using a NULL terminated list of arguments and an array of pointers to the environment entries. When the command completes, the program resumes control.

spawnlp

Syntax: int spawnlp(int *invoke_flag*, char *pathname*, char *arg0*, char
  arg1, ..., NULL);
Include file: <process.h>
Executes the specified DOS command (child process), using a NULL terminated list of arguments and searching for the command in the directories specified by the PATH environment variable. When the command completes, the program resumes control.

spawnlpe
Syntax: int spawnlpe(int *invoke_flag*, char **pathname*, char **arg0*,
  char **arg1*, ..., NULL, char **envp*[]);
Include file: <process.h>
Executes the specified DOS command (child process), using a NULL terminated list of arguments and an array of pointers to the environment entries; searches for the command in the directories specified by the PATH environment variable. When the command completes, the program resumes control.

spawnv
Syntax: int spawnv(int *invoke_flag*, char **pathname*, char **argv*[]);
Include file: <process.h>
Executes the specified DOS command (child process), using an array of pointers to the command line arguments. When the command completes, the program resumes control.

spawnve
Syntax: int spawnve(int *invoke_flag*, char **pathname*, char **argv*[],
  char **envp*[]);
Include file: <process.h>
Executes the specified DOS command (child process), using an array of pointers to the command line arguments and an array of pointers to the environment entries. When the command completes, the program resumes control.

spawnvp
Syntax: int spawnvp(int *invoke_flag*, char **pathname*, char **argv*[]);
Include file: <process.h>
Executes the specified DOS command (child process), using an array of pointers to the command line arguments and searching for the command in the directories specified by the PATH environment variable. When the command completes, the program resumes control.

spawnvpe
Syntax: int spawnvpe(int *invoke_flag*, char **pathname*, char **argv*[],
  char **envp*[]);
Include file: <process.h>
Executes the specified DOS command (child process), using an array of pointers to the command line arguments and an array of pointers to the environment entries; searches for the command in the directories specified by the PATH environment variable. When the command completes, the program resumes control.

_splitpath
Syntax: void _splitpath(char *pathname*, char *drive*, char *subdirectory*, char *filename*, char *extension*);
Include file: <stdlib.h>
Breaks a complete DOS pathname into a disk drive letter, a subdirectory path, a filename, and an extension.

sprintf
Syntax: int sprintf(char *buffer*, const char *format_specification*,[,*argument*...]);
Include file: <stdio.h>
Writes output formatting of a sequence of characters to a character string buffer rather than to an output device or to a file.

sqrt
Syntax: double sqrt(double *expression*);
Include file: <math.h>
Returns the square root of the specified numeric expression.

srand
Syntax: void srand(unsigned *seed*);
Include file: <stdlib.h>
Uses the specified seed to assign a starting value to the random number generator.

sscanf
Syntax: int sscanf(const char *buffer*, const char *format_specification*[, &*argument*...]);
Include file: <stdio.h>
Reads formatted input operations from a character string rather than from an input device or from a file; reads into the locations given by the arguments.

stackavail
Syntax: size_t stackavail(void);
Include file: <malloc.h>
Returns the approximate number of bytes of stack space available for dynamic allocation using the *alloca()* function.

stat
Syntax: int stat(char *pathname*, struct stat *file_info*);
Include file: <sys\stat.h>
Returns information about the specified file.

_status87
Syntax: unsigned int _status87(void);
Include file: <float.h>
Returns the word containing the floating-point status.

strcat
Syntax: char *strcat(char *target*, const char **source*);
Include file: <string.h>
Appends the source string to the target string.

strchr
Syntax: char *strchr(const char *string*, char *letter*);
Include file: <string.h>
Searches a string for the first occurrence of the specified character.

strcmp
Syntax: int strcmp(const char *string1*, const char *string2*);
Include file: <string.h>
Compares two character strings.

strcmpi
Syntax: int strcmpi(const char *string1*, const char *string2*);
Include file: <string.h>
Compares two strings, ignoring the case of each letter.

strcpy
Syntax: char *strcpy(char *target*, const char *source*);
Include file: <string.h>
Copies the contents of the source character string to the target string and returns the target string.

strcspn
Syntax: size_t strcspn(const char *string*, const char *substring*);
Include file: <string.h>
Returns the index of the first occurrence of a substring within a string.

_strdate
Syntax: char *_strdate(char *date*);
Include file: <time.h>
Assigns the current date to the specified character string buffer.

strdup
Syntax: char *strdup(const char *source*);
Include file: <string.h>
Allocates storage for a string and copies the contents of the source string to the storage space, returning a pointer to the string.

strerror
Syntax: char *strerror(int *error_number*);
Include file: <string.h>
Returns the error message that corresponds to the specified error number.

_strerror
Syntax: char *_strerror(char *str*);
Include file: <string.h>
Returns a character string that contains the error message associated with the *errno* global variable, which holds the status value for the last error produced by a library function.

stricmp
Syntax: int stricmp(const char *string1*, const char *string2*);
Include file: <string.h>
Compares two character strings, ignoring the case of each letter.

strlen
Syntax: int strlen(const char *str*);
Include file: <string.h>
Returns the number of bytes that are used in a NULL terminated character string.

strlwr
Syntax: char *strlwr(char *str*);
Include file: <string.h>
Converts a character string's uppercase letters to lowercase.

strncat
Syntax: char *strncat(char *target*, const char *source*, size_t *num_bytes*);
Include file: <string.h>
Appends *num_bytes* characters of the source string to the specified target string.

strncmp
Syntax: int strncmp(const char *string1*, const char *string2*, size_t *num_bytes*);
Include file: <string.h>
Compares the first *num_bytes* characters of two character strings.

strncpy
Syntax: char *strncpy(char *target*, char *source*, int *num_bytes*);
Include file: <string.h>
Copies the first *num_bytes* characters from the source string to the target.

strnicmp
Syntax: int strnicmp(const char *string1*, const char *string2*, int *num_bytes*);
Include file: <string.h>
Compares the first *num_bytes* characters of two character strings, ignoring the case of each letter.

strnset
Syntax: char *strnset(char *string*, int *letter*, size_t *num_bytes*);
Include file: <string.h>
Assigns the specified character to the first *num_bytes* characters of a string.

strpbrk
Syntax: char *strpbrk(const char *string1*, const char *string2*);
Include file: <string.h>
Returns a pointer to the first occurrence of a character that is contained in the first string that is equal to any character in the second string.

strrchr
Syntax: char *strrchr(const char *str*, int *letter*);
Include file: <string.h>
Returns a pointer to the rightmost occurrence of the specified character in a string.

strrev
Syntax: char *strrev(char *str*);
Include file: <string.h>
Reverses the order of characters in a string.

strset
Syntax: char *strset(char *str*, int *letter*);
Include file: <string.h>
Sets all characters in a string, up to the NULL character, to the specified letter.

strspn
Syntax: size_t strspn(const char *string1*, const char *string2*);
Include file: <string.h>
Returns the index position of the first character in the first string that is not in the second string.

strstr
Syntax: char *strstr(const char *string*, const char *substring*);
Include file: <string.h>
Returns a pointer to the first occurrence of a substring within a string.

_strtime
Syntax: char *_strtime(char *time*);
Include file: <time.h>
Assigns the current system time to the specified character string buffer.

strtod
Syntax: double strtod(const char *str*, char **endscan*);
Include file: <stdlib.h>
Converts a character string representation of a value to a double-precision value.

strtok
Syntax: char *strtok(char *str*, const char *tokens*);
Include file: <string.h>
Returns a pointer to the location of a specific token in a string.

strtol
Syntax: long strtol(const char *str*, char **endscan*, int *radix*);
Include file: <stdlib.h>
Converts a character string representation of a value to a long integer, using the specified radix (base).

strtoul
Syntax: unsigned long strtoul(const char *str*, char **endscan*, int *radix*);
Include file: <stdlib.h>
Converts a character string representation of a number to an unsigned long integer, using the specified radix (base).

strupr

Syntax: char *strupr(char *str);
Include file: <string.h>
Converts a character string's lowercase letters to uppercase.

swab

Syntax: void swab(char *source, char *target, int num_bytes);
Include file: <stdlib.h>
Swaps adjacent bytes of the first *num_bytes* bytes of a buffer, assigning the result to a target buffer.

system

Syntax: int system(const char *command);
Include files: <stdlib.h>, <process.h>
Executes the DOS command that is specified by the *command* character string.

tan

Syntax: double tan(double *expression*);
Include file: <math.h>
Returns the tangent of a numeric expression.

tanh

Syntax: double tanh(double *expression*)
Include file: <math.h>
Returns the hyperbolic tangent of a numeric expression.

tell

Syntax: long tell(int *file_handle*);
Include file: <io.h>
Returns the current file pointer offset for the file that is associated with the specified handle.

tempnam

Syntax: char *tempnam(char *directory*, char *prefix*);
Include file: <stdio.h>
Creates a unique file that has the specified prefix in the subdirectory that is defined by the TMP environment variable or in the specified subdirectory if TMP is not defined. If TMP is not defined and if the directory associated with TMP does not exist, *tempnam()* creates the file in the directory that is associated with the *P_tmpdir* variable. That variable is found in the stdio.h include file. If *P_tmpdir* is not defined, *tempnam()* creates the file in the current working directory.

time
Syntax: time_t time(time_t *current_time*);
Include file: <time.h>
Determines the current time, returning the number of seconds since midnight 01/01/1970 Greenwich mean time.

tmpfile
Syntax: FILE *tmpfile(void);
Include file: <stdio.h>
Creates a temporary file and returns a file pointer to that file.

tmpnam
Syntax: char *tmpnam(char *unique_name*);
Include file: <stdio.h>
Creates and returns a unique filename in the subdirectory that is defined by the *P_tmpdir* variable in the stdio.h include file.

toascii
Syntax: int toascii(int *letter*);
Include file: <ctype.h>
Converts an integer value to an ASCII character by clearing all but the value's seven least significant bits.

tolower, _tolower
Syntax: int tolower(int *letter*);   /* tests for uppercase */
Syntax: int _tolower(int *letter*); /* does not test for uppercase */
Include file: <ctype.h>
Converts an uppercase letter to lowercase. The *tolower()* function first tests to ensure that the letter is an uppercase letter. The *tolower()* function is also found in the stdlib.h include file. The *_tolower()* macro does not test the letter for uppercase.

toupper, _toupper
Syntax: int toupper(int *letter*);   /* tests for lowercase */
Syntax: int _toupper(int *letter*); /* does not test for lowercase */
Include file: <ctype.h>
Converts a lowercase letter to uppercase. The *toupper()* function first tests to ensure that the letter is a lowercase letter. The *toupper()* function is also found in the stdlib.h include file. The *_toupper()* macro does not test the letter for lowercase.

tzset
Syntax: void tzset(void);
Include file: <time.h>
Assigns values to the *daylight*, *timezone*, and *tzname* global variables, using the current setting for the TZ environment variable.

ultoa
Syntax: char *ultoa(unsigned long *value*, char *ascii*, int *radix*);
Include file: <stdlib.h>
Converts an unsigned long value to its ASCII representation, using the specified radix (base).

umask
Syntax: int umask(int *permission*);
Include file: <io.h>
Sets the program's file permission mask. The *permission* parameter must be one or both of the following:

S_IREAD   Reading not allowed
S_IWRITE   Write access not allowed

ungetc
Syntax: int ungetc(int *letter*, FILE *file_pointer*);
Include file: <stdio.h>
Returns a character to the specified input stream for later input processing.

ungetch
Syntax: int ungetch(int *letter*);
Include file: <conio.h>
Returns a character from stdin to the specified input stream for later input processing. The next character read from the console will be the character placed there by *ungetch()*.

unlink
Syntax: int unlink(const char *pathname*);
Include files: <io.h>, <stdio.h>
Deletes the specified file from the disk.

_unregisterfonts
Syntax: void far _unregisterfonts(void);
Include file:<graph.h>
Unloads the currently selected font data from memory and frees memory allocated and used by the *_registerfonts()* function.

utime
Syntax: int utime(char *pathname*, struct utimbuf *stamp*);
Include file: <sys\utime.h>
Sets a file's time stamp.

va_arg
Syntax: va_arg(va_list *argument_ptr*, *type*);
Include files: <stdarg.h>, <varargs.h>

Returns the next argument in a variable-length list of parameters. The *va_arg()* function works in conjunction with the *va_start()* function to access parameters that are passed to functions in a list that contains a variable number of parameters.

va_end
Syntax: void va_end(va_list *argument_ptr*);
Include files: <stdarg.h>, <varargs.h>
Sets the argument pointer that the *va_arg()* function uses to NULL after the function has retrieved the last argument in a variable-length list of arguments.

va_start
Syntax: void va_start(va_list *argument_ptr*); or void va_start(va_list *argument_ptr*, *previous_parameter*); /* ANSI */
Include files: <stdarg.h>, <varargs.h>
Sets the argument pointer to the first parameter in a variable-length list of arguments to a function.

vfprintf
Syntax: int vfprintf(FILE *file_pointer*, const char *format_specification*, va_list *argument_ptr*);
Include file: <stdio.h>
Writes formatted output to a file, using a variable number of parameters.

vprintf
Syntax: int vprintf(const char *format_specification*, va_list *argument_ptr*);
Include file: <stdio.h>
Writes formatted output to stdout, using a variable number of parameters.

vsprintf
Syntax: int vsprintf(char *buffer*, const char *format_specification*, va_list *argument_ptr*);
Include file: <stdio.h>
Writes formatted output to a character string, using a variable number of parameters.

_wrapon
Syntax: short far *_wrapon(short *wrapflag*);
Include file: <graph.h>
Controls whether the text output written to an output window by the *_outtext()* function is wrapped or truncated when it reaches the window's right margin:

_GWRAPON   Text wrapped within the window
_GWRAPOFF   Text truncated

write

Syntax: int write(int *file_handle*, char **buffer*, unsigned *num_bytes*);
Include file: <io.h>
Writes the number of specified bytes from a buffer to the file specified by *file_handle*.

4: *QuickC Compiler Error Messages*

The following sections explain each error message and warning message that the QuickC compiler generates. Each compiler error is presented in the form shown below:

Error #   **Error Message**

The text below the message then describes the cause of the error in more detail.

Fatal error messages

The messages below identify fatal compiler errors. The QuickC compiler displays the error message and then terminates; it cannot recover from a fatal error.

C1000   **UNKNOWN FATAL ERROR**
Contact Microsoft Technical Support

The compiler detected an error that it was not able to handle or to recover from. If you cannot determine what caused the error, call Microsoft's Product Support Services group at (206) 454-2030.

C1001   **Internal Compiler Error**
(compiler file '*filename*', line *n*)
Contact Microsoft Technical Support

The compiler detected an error in one of its internal files. For help, call Microsoft's Product Support Services group at (206) 454-2030.

C1002   **out of heap space**

The compiler did not have sufficient dynamic memory (heap space) to continue. This error is common in programs that use a large number of identifiers or complex expressions. If possible, break your program into smaller modules and compile each independently, linking the object files to create your executable program.

C1003   **error count exceeds** *n*; **stopping compilation**

The compiler encountered so many errors that it cannot continue. This error often occurs when you have forgotten to close a comment or when you have omitted a function's closing brace.

C1004   **unexpected EOF**

The compiler encountered the end of your source file when it expected additional statements. This situation normally occurs when you forget to close a comment or when you use an #if preprocessor directive without following it with the #endif directive.

C1007   **unrecognized flag '***flag***' in '***command-option***'**

The command line contained an invalid option. For information about compiler options, see "The QCL compiler" in Section 1 and "Compiling" in Section 2 of this quick reference.

C1008   **no input file specified**

The command line called the compiler without specifying a source file to compile. Type the QCL command again, and include the source file's name.

C1009   **compiler limit : macros too deeply nested**

The preprocessor could not expand the specified macro because of multiple levels of nesting. Check the macro to verify that it does not refer to itself recursively.

C1010   **compiler limit : macro expansion too big**

A macro's expansion exceeded the space that is available. The QuickC compiler restricts a macro's expansion size to 1024 bytes.

C1011   **compiler limit : '***identifier***' : macro definition too big**

QuickC supports macros of up to 1024 bytes, and the given macro exceeded this limit. If possible, break the macro into smaller macros.

C1012   **bad parenthesis nesting - missing '***character***'**

The preprocessor detected a missing parenthesis in a preprocessor directive. The specified character can be either a left or a right parenthesis.

C1013 cannot open source file '*filename*'

The compiler was unable to open the specified source file for compilation. Check your spelling of the source filename. Use the DIR command to ensure that the specified file exists. Last, verify that the FILES entry in your CONFIG.SYS file is set to at least 20.

C1014 too many include files

The QuickC compiler restricts the nesting of include files to 10 levels, and the nesting exceeded that limit. If possible, reduce the number of include files by creating modules that you can compile independently and then link those files to create the executable file.

C1015 cannot open include file '*filename*'

The preprocessor could not open the specified include file. Check your spelling of the include file's name. Use the DIR command to ensure that the specified file exists. Last, verify that the FILES entry in your CONFIG.SYS file is set to at least 20.

C1016 #if[n]def expected an identifier

The preprocessor encountered an #ifdef or an #ifndef preprocessor directive that did not include an identifier. Edit the file either by specifying an identifier to test for or by removing the directive that caused the error.

C1017 invalid integer constant expression

An #if directive contained an expression that did not evaluate to a constant. The #if preprocessor directive supports only integer constants.

C1018 unexpected '#elif'

The preprocessor encountered an #elif preprocessor directive without a corresponding #if, #ifdef, or #ifndef directive. In many cases, this error occurs when you fail to close a comment.

C1019 unexpected '#else'

The preprocessor encountered an #else preprocessor directive without a corresponding #if, #ifdef, or #ifndef directive. In many cases, this error occurs when you fail to close a comment.

C1020 **unexpected '#endif'**

The preprocessor encountered an #endif preprocessor directive without a corresponding #if, #ifdef, or #ifndef directive. In many cases, this error occurs when you fail to close a comment.

C1021 **bad preprocessor command '*string*'**

The string of characters following a pound sign (#) did not create a valid preprocessor directive. For information about these directives, see ''Preprocessor directives'' in Section 2 of this quick reference.

C1022 **expected '#endif'**

The preprocessor encountered an #if, an #ifdef, or an #ifndef preprocessor directive without the corresponding #endif preprocessor directive. In many cases, this error occurs when you fail to close a comment. For information about these directives, see ''Preprocessor directives'' in Section 2 of this quick reference.

C1025 **compiler terminated by user**

The user stopped the compiler.

C1028 *segment* **segment allocation exceeds 64K**

The amount of space allocated for far data exceeded 64 KB. If possible, break your declarations into separate modules that you can compile independently and then link those files to create the executable file.

C1031 **compiler limit : function calls too deeply nested**

The function calls within the program were nested at too many levels. The compiler cannot continue.

C1032 **cannot open object listing file '*filename*'**

The compiler could not create the specified object file listing because one of the following existed:

   The specified filename is invalid.

   The file with the specified filename cannot be opened because of insufficient disk space.

   The file with the specified filename already exists on disk and is marked read-only.

C1035 **expression too complex, please simplify**

An expression was too complex for the compiler to evaluate. If possible, break the expression into smaller expressions and then combine the result as necessary.

C1037 **cannot open object file '***filename***'**

The compiler could not create the specified object file because one of the following existed:

> The specified filename is invalid.
>
> The file with the specified filename cannot be opened because of insufficient disk space.
>
> The specified filename already exists on disk and is marked read-only.

C1041 **cannot open compiler intermediate file - no more files**

The compiler could not create an intermediate file needed for compilation because no more file handles existed. Verify that the FILES entry in your CONFIG.SYS file is set to at least 20.

C1045 **floating point overflow**

The compiler encountered a floating-point overflow while working with a floating-point constant. Examine the expression that caused the error and, if possible, use a double-precision variable.

C1047 **too many** *option* **flags, '***string***'**

The specified option in the string occurred too many times, and the compiler could not continue.

C1048 **unknown option '***character***' in '***string***'**

The specified character was invalid for the option string displayed, and the compiler could not continue.

C1049 **invalid numeric argument '***string***'**

The compiler encountered a character string when it expected a numeric argument.

C1052 **too many #if/#ifdef's**

QuickC restricts the number of nested #if/#ifdef preprocessor directives to 32 levels, and the program exceeded that limit.

C1053 **compiler limit : struct/union nesting**

QuickC restricts the number of nested structures to 10, and the program exceeded that limit.

C1054 **compiler limit : initializers too deeply nested**

QuickC restricts the level of initializing nesting to 15, and the program exceeded that limit.

C1055 **compiler limit : out of keys**

The number of symbols your program can reference is dependent upon the amount of dynamic memory that is available, and the program exceeded the compiler's storage capacity. If possible, break the program into smaller modules that you can compile separately.

C1056 **compiler limit : out of macro expansion space**

The expansion of a macro overflowed one of the compiler's internal buffers. If possible, shorten the macro to reduce the size of the expansion.

C1059 **out of near heap space**

The compiler ran out of storage space in the default data segment (near heap). If possible, break the program into smaller modules that you can compile separately.

C1060 **out of far heap space**

The compiler ran out of storage space in the far heap. If you are compiling the program from within the QuickC environment, disable debugging to reduce the number of symbols that QuickC defines. If you are compiling the program from the command line, you might have to remove memory-resident programs before you can proceed.

C1061 **compiler limit : blocks too deeply nested**

A block is a section of code that is enclosed within an opening and closing brace, and a nested block is a block within a second block (such as a *while* statement within an *if* statement). In this case, the program exceeded the number of nested blocks that QuickC supports. If possible, break the program into separate functions that perform the same processing as the nested blocks.

C1062 **error writing to preprocessor output file**

The compiler command line contained the /E, /P, or /EP option, and the disk had insufficient space for the preprocessor file. Remove unnecessary files from the disk, and type the QCL command again.

C1063 **compiler limit : compiler stack overflow**

The program code was too complex for the compiler, resulting in a stack overflow. If possible, simplify the code by creating simpler functions.

C1064 **compiler limit : identifier overflowed internal buffer**

An identifier exceeded the length of the internal compiler buffer used for identifiers. If possible, use a shorter identifier name and recompile.

C1068 **cannot open file '*filename*'**

The compiler could not open the specified file. Verify that the FILES entry in your CONFIG.SYS file is set to at least 20.

C1069 **write error on file '*filename*'**

The QuickC compiler could not complete its output to the specified file. Remove unnecessary files from the disk, and try compiling again.

C1070 **mismatched #if/#endif pair in file '*filename*'**

The preprocessor encountered an #if, #ifdef, or #ifndef preprocessor directive without the corresponding #endif directive.

C1126 *identifier*: **automatic allocation exceeds '*size*'**

The size of a local variable exceeded the space limit that the QuickC compiler imposes. If possible, reduce the size of the specified identifier and recompile.

Compilation error messages

The following messages show errors in your programs. After encountering any of these errors, the compiler continues parsing the program if possible and displays additional error messages. The compiler does not, however, produce an object file.

C2000 **UNKNOWN ERROR**
Contact Microsoft Technical Support

The compiler detected an error that it could not identify. If you cannot determine what caused the error, call Microsoft's Product Support Services at (206) 454-2030.

C2001 **newline in constant**

A newline character ('\n') was not in the correct format.

C2003 **expected 'defined id'**

The preprocessor encountered an #if preprocessor directive without an identifier.

C2004 **expected 'defined(id)'**

The syntax associated with an #if defined preprocessor directive was invalid. The #if defined (*identifier*) directive requires an identifier. Correct the syntax and recompile.

C2005 **#line expected a line number, found '*string*'**

A #line preprocessor directive did not include the required line number. Change the first value after the #line directive to make it a numeric line number. The format of the #line directive is *#line nnn filename,* where *nnn* is the value that the preprocessor assigns to its internal line counter.

C2006 **#include expected a file name, found '*string*'**

The specified #include preprocessor directive did not contain a filename in the correct format. #include lets you group the filename within either brackets (<>) or double quotation marks.

C2007 **#define syntax**

The syntax associated with the specified #define preprocessor directive was invalid. The format for the #define directive is *#define identifier value*. Correct the statement and recompile.

C2008 **'*character*' : unexpected in macro definition**

A macro used the specified character incorrectly. Correct the macro definition and recompile.

C2009   **reuse of macro formal '***identifier***'**

The specified identifier occurred more than one time in a macro definition's formal parameters. The formal parameters are those parameters that are separated by commas and that the preprocessor later expands to values.

C2010   **'***character***' : unexpected in formal list**

The specified character occurred unexpectedly in a macro's formal parameter list. The formal parameters must be valid C identifiers.

C2012   **missing name following '<'**

The preprocessor encountered an #include preprocessor directive that did not contain a filename following the open bracket. The #include preprocessor directive lets you include a filename within either brackets (<>) or double quotation marks.

C2013   **missing '>'**

The preprocessor encountered an #include preprocessor directive that included a file but did not include the closing bracket after the filename. Add the closing bracket and recompile.

C2014   **preprocessor command must start as first non-whitespace**

The preprocessor encountered a preprocessor directive that did not contain the first non-whitespace characters on the line. Edit your program so that your preprocessor directives start in column one.

C2015   **too many chars in constant**

A character constant contained more than one character or escape sequence. Character constants appear in single quotation marks; character strings appear in double quotation marks. Correct the error and recompile.

C2016   **no closing single quote**

The compiler encountered a character constant that did not include the closing single quotation mark. Correct the error and recompile.

C2017   **illegal escape sequence**

Following a backslash (\), the compiler encountered a character that was not a valid escape sequence character.

See "printf control sequences" in Section 2 of this quick reference for a table of valid escape sequences.

C2018 **unknown character '0x***character***'**

The specified hexadecimal value did not correspond to a valid character. Characters can store values in the range 0 through 0xFF.

C2019 **expected preprocessor command, found '***character***'**

The preprocessor encountered a pound sign followed by a character, but that character was not the first letter of a preprocessor directive.

C2021 **expected exponent value, not '***character***'**

The QuickC compiler expected the numeric value to be used for the exponent of a floating-point constant. Instead, the compiler encountered the specified illegal character.

C2022 **'***number***' : too big for char**

The specified number is outside the variable type's range. A variable of type *char* can store values in the range −128 through 127. A variable of type *unsigned char* can store values in the range 0 through 255.

C2023 **divide by 0**

During compilation, the denominator of a division operation was 0. Division by 0 results in an undefined expression.

C2024 **mod by 0**

During compilation, the second operand in a modulus operation was 0. The modulus operator (%) returns the remainder of a division, and division by 0 results in an undefined expression.

C2025 **'***identifier***' : enum/struct/union type redefinition**

The specified identifier was already used in a definition for an enumeration, a structure, or a union tag. Tag identifiers must be unique.

C2026 **'***identifier***' : member of enum redefinition**

The specified identifier was already used as an enumerated constant. Enumerated type names must be distinct.

C2027 **use of undefined enum/struct/union '*identifier*'**

The specified identifier referred to a structure or a union type that was not defined. If you are using a structure or a union that C defines, be sure that you included the correct include files.

C2028 **struct/union member needs to be inside a struct/union**

The compiler encountered a structure or a union member that was not in a structure or a union. This error occurs most often when you try to specify a type before one or more of the constants in an enumerated type. When you do so, the enumeration takes on the look of a structure or a union. Enumerated constants are of type *unsigned int*.

C2029 **'*identifier*' : bit-fields allowed only in structs**

The compiler encountered a declaration of bit fields not contained in a structure. Only structure types can contain bit fields for their members.

C2030 **'*identifier*' : struct/union member redefinition**

Each member in a structure or a union must have a unique name. In this case, a member identifier appeared twice in the same structure or union.

C2031 **'*identifier*' : function cannot be struct/union member**

A function cannot be a member of a structure or a union. Instead, use a pointer to a function.

C2032 **'*identifier*' : base type with near/far/huge not allowed**

C does not support structure members whose types include the *near*, *far*, or *huge* keyword.

C2033 **'*identifier*' : bit-field cannot have indirection**

The specified bit field was declared as a pointer (∗*member*). C does not support pointers to bit fields.

C2034 **'*identifier*' : bit-field type too small for number of bits**

The specified number of bits in a bit-field declaration was greater than the available number of bits for the specified type. An *unsigned int* value can store 16 bits.

C2035 **struct/union '*identifier*' : unknown size**

The compiler could not determine the size of a structure or a union based on the declaration. Edit the structure, verifying that each member is a specific size.

C2036　　left of '*identifier*' must have struct/union type

An expression used either the dot (.) or the –> operator to reference a member. The variable to the left of the operator was not a structure or a union.

C2037　　struct/union left of '*operator*' specifies undefined '*identifier*'

An expression used either the dot (.) or the –> operator to reference a member. The variable to the left of the operator was not defined.

C2038　　'*identifier*' : not struct/union member

An expression used the specified identifier in the context of a structure or a union member. But the identifier was not a member. This error usually occurs when you misspell a member name.

C2039　　'–>' requires struct/union pointer

An expression used the –> member selection operator. The variable before the operator was not a pointer to a structure or a union. If you use pointers to structures, use the –> operator to access a structure member. If you use structures, use the dot (.) operator.

C2040　　'.' requires struct/union name

An expression used the dot (.) member selection operator, but the variable before the operator was a pointer to a structure or a union, and not a structure or a union.

C2041　　illegal digit '*character*' for base '*number*'

The character value shown was not a valid digit for the specified numeric base. Octal values can store digits in the range 0 through 7. Hexadecimal values can store digits in the range 0 through F.

C2042　　signed/unsigned keywords mutually exclusive

A variable declaration used both the *signed* and *unsigned* type qualifiers. A variable must be either *signed* or *unsigned*; it cannot be both.

C2043　　illegal break

The compiler encountered a *break* statement that was not within a *for*, *while*, *do*, or *switch* statement.

C2044 **illegal continue**

The compiler encountered a *continue* statement that was not within a *for*, *while*, or *do* statement.

C2045 **'*identifier*' : label redefined**

The specified label appeared more than once in the same function. A label marks a specific location in your function that the *goto* statement can branch to. Each location must have a unique name.

C2046 **illegal case**

The compiler encountered a *case* statement outside a *switch* statement. The *case* statement can be used only within a *switch* statement.

C2047 **illegal default**

The compiler encountered a *default* statement outside a *switch* statement. The *default* statement can be used only within a *switch* statement.

C2048 **more than one default**

The compiler encountered more than one *default* statement in a *switch* statement. A *switch* statement can have only one *default* statement.

C2050 **non-integral switch expression**

The compiler encountered a nonintegral *switch* expression. The expression that the *switch* statement evaluates must result in an integer value.

C2051 **case expression not constant**

The compiler encountered a *case* statement expression that was not a constant. The expressions for each *case* statement within a *switch* statement must result in a constant value. You cannot use a variable for a *case* expression.

C2052 **case expression not integral**

The compiler encountered a *case* statement expression that was not integral. The expression for a *case* statement within a *switch* statement must result in an integer constant. The switch statement supports only integer expressions.

C2053 **case value *number* already used**

An expression that was equal to another expression appeared earlier in the *switch* statement. The expressions for each case in a *switch* statement must result in a unique number.

C2054 **expected '(' to follow '*identifier*'**

Using the specified identifier requires a parenthesis to signify a list of parameters.

C2055 **expected formal parameter list, not a type list**

The QuickC compiler expected to find the formal parameter list to be used by a function but instead encountered a type list. Verify that you specified the name of each variable in the formal parameter list.

C2056 **illegal expression**

A previous syntax error has made the specified expression illegal.

C2057 **expected constant expression**

The QuickC compiler expected an expression that results in a constant value (e.g., the number of elements in an array) but instead encountered an expression that does not result in a constant.

C2058 **constant expression is not integral**

The QuickC compiler expected an expression that results in a constant integer value (e.g., the number of elements in an array) but instead encountered an expression that does not result in an integer value.

C2059 **syntax error : '*token*'**

The specified token (or symbol) was invalid.

C2060 **syntax error : EOF**

The QuickC compiler encountered an end of file unexpectedly, which signifies that the source file is incomplete. The file might be missing either statements or closing braces.

C2061 **syntax error : identifier '*identifier*'**

The specified identifier was invalid.

C2062 **type '*type*' unexpected**

The specified *type* was misused in a declaration.

C2063 **'*identifier*' : not a function**

The program does not declare the identifier as a function but attempts to use it as such. This error usually occurs when you misspell a function name.

C2064 **term does not evaluate to a function**

The program attempted to call a function using an expression that results in a function pointer, but the expression did not result in a valid function pointer.

C2065 **'*identifier*' : undefined**

The program referenced a variable that has not been defined.

C2066 **cast to function returning...is illegal**

C does not let you cast an expression to a function.

C2067 **cast to array type is illegal**

C does not let you cast an expression to an array type. Instead, cast the result to a pointer.

C2068 **illegal cast**

The type that was specified in a cast operation was not a valid type.

C2069 **cast of 'void' term to non-void**

C does not let you cast an expression of type *void* to a nonvoid type. An expression of type *void* does not return a value, so you cannot cast its result.

C2070 **illegal sizeof operand**

The operand in a *sizeof* operation must be a valid identifier or type name.

C2071 **'*identifier*' : bad storage class**

The specified storage class modifier could not be used in this context. For information about storage class modifiers, see ''Types'' in Section 2 of this quick reference.

C2072   *'identifier'* : **initialization of function**

The program tried to assign a value to an identifier that is associated with a function.

C2075   *'identifier'* : **array initialization needs curly braces**

An array declaration tried to initialize the elements of the array without using braces ({}) to group the initial values. The correct declaration format is as follows:

```
static int array[5] = {1, 2, 3, 4, 5};
```

C does not let you initialize automatic arrays. As a result, the array declaration includes the *static* storage class modifier.

C2076   *'identifier'* : **struct/union initialization needs curly braces**

A structure or union declaration tried to initialize the members without using braces ({}) to group the initial values. The correct declaration format is as follows:

```
struct coords
    {
    int x;
    int y;
    };
static struct coords box = {10, 20};
```

C2077   **non-scalar field initializer** *'identifier'*

The specified expression tried to initialize a bit field member with a nonscalar value.

C2078   **too many initializers**

A variable declaration tried to initialize the variable. In this case, the number of initial values exceeded the number of array elements or structure members to be initialized.

C2079   *'identifier'* **uses undefined struct/union** *'name'*

A variable declaration tried to declare a structure or a union whose type is unknown to the compiler. If you use a type defined by C, be sure that you used the correct include files.

C2082   **redefinition of formal parameter '***identifier***'**

A local variable declaration in a function used an identifier name that appeared previously in the function's list of formal parameters. Be sure that the identifier names you use are unique.

C2084   **function '***identifier***' already has a body**

The specified function was already defined in the program. To reduce possible confusion as you examine your source code, be sure that the function names you use are unique.

C2085   **'***identifier***' : not in formal parameter list**

An identifier declared in a function definition was not declared in the formal parameter list declaration.

C2086   **'***identifier***' : redefinition**

The specified identifier was defined more than once. Identifiers for local variables or functions must be unique.

C2087   **'***identifier***' : missing subscript**

The specified array is a multidimensional array and is missing the subscript value for one of its dimensions (other than the first dimension).

C2090   **function returns array**

A function must not return an array. Have the function return a pointer to an array instead.

C2091   **function returns function**

A function must not return a function. Have the function return a pointer to a function instead.

C2092   **array element type cannot be function**

An array cannot store functions. Have the array store pointers to functions instead.

C2093   **cannot initialize a static or struct with address of automatic vars**

The QuickC compiler does not let you initialize a static variable, such as a pointer, using the address of an automatic variable.

C2094   **label '***identifier***' was undefined**

A *goto* statement within a function referenced a label that is not defined within the function.

C2095   *function* **: actual has type void : parameter** *number*

A formal parameter cannot be declared as type *void*. A pointer to a parameter of type *void* (*void* ∗) is valid.

C2096   **struct/union comparison illegal**

C does not let you compare two structures or unions. Compare the corresponding members individually instead.

C2097   **illegal initialization**

A declaration tried to initialize a variable using a nonconstant value.

C2098   **non-address expression**

An expression tried to initialize an identifier that was not an lvalue. An lvalue is an expression, such as an identifier, that refers to a region of memory.

C2099   **non-constant offset**

An initializer used a nonconstant offset value.

C2100   **illegal indirection**

An expression tried to use the indirection operator (∗) with a nonpointer value.

C2101   **'&' on constant**

An expression tried to use the address operator (&) with a constant.

C2102   **'&' requires lvalue**

An expression tried to use the address operator (&) with an operand that is not an lvalue. An lvalue is an expression, such as an identifier, that refers to a region of memory.

C2103   **'&' on register variable**

An expression tried to use the address operator (&) with a variable that is declared with the *register* storage class modifier.

C2104 **'&' on bit-field ignored**

An expression tried to use the address operator (&) to find the address of a bit field.

C2105 *'operator'* **needs lvalue**

The specified operator requires an lvalue. An lvalue is an expression, such as an identifier, that refers to a region of memory.

C2106 *'operator'* **: left operand must be lvalue**

The operand to the left of the specified operator must be an lvalue. An lvalue is an expression, such as an identifier, that refers to a region of memory.

C2107 **illegal index, indirection not allowed**

An expression that did not result in a pointer tried to use a subscript. C allows you to subscript only arrays and pointer values.

C2108 **non-integral index**

A statement tried to use an index value that did not result in an integer value. C supports only integral array indexes.

C2109 **subscript on non-array**

A statement tried to use a subscript on a variable that is not an array. C lets you subscript only arrays and pointer values.

C2110 **'+' : 2 pointers**

An expression tried to add one pointer value to another. C allows you to add offset values to a pointer, but you cannot add one pointer to another.

C2111 **pointer + non-integral value**

An expression tried to add an expression to a pointer that did not evaluate to an integer value. Offsets to pointers must be integral values.

C2112 **illegal pointer subtraction**

An expression tried to subtract two pointers that did not point to values of the same type. C allows you to subtract pointer values, but the pointers must reference the same type.

C2113 **'−' : right operand pointer**

An expression tried to subtract a pointer from a value that was not a pointer. C allows you to subtract pointer values, but the pointers must reference the same type. In this case, only the right operand was a pointer.

C2114 **'*operator*' : pointer on left; needs integral right**

An expression tried to perform an operation on a pointer value. The operand on the right side of the operator must be an integer value.

C2115 **'*identifier*' : incompatible types**

An expression tried to manipulate types that are incompatible.

C2116 **'*operator*' : bad '*direction*' operand**

The left or right operand for the specified operator was invalid. See "Operators" in Section 2 of this quick reference.

C2117 **'*operator*' : illegal for struct/union**

The specified operator cannot be used on a structure or a union. This error usually occurs when you forget to specify a member name.

C2118 **negative subscript**

A declaration tried to define an array of negative size. The lowest array subscript that C supports is 0.

C2119 **'typedefs' both define indirection**

A declaration used two type names created by the *typedef* statement, and both *typedef* statements used indirection. C does not support this double indirection.

C2120 **'void' illegal with all types**

A declaration of another type tried to use *void*. Variables can be void pointers (*void* ∗), but variables cannot be of type *void*.

C2125 **'*identifier*' : allocation exceeds 64K**

The specified identifier tried to allocate more than 64 KB of memory.

C2127 **parameter allocation exceeds 32K**

QuickC restricts the size of function parameters to 32 KB.

C2130   **#line expected a string containing the file name, found** '*string*'

The #line preprocessor directive lets you specify both a line number for the preprocessor's internal line counter and a filename. In this case, the directive did not contain a filename.

C2131   **attributes specify more than one near/far/huge**

A variable declaration tried to use more than one of the *near*, *far*, and *huge* type qualifiers. A variable can use only one of the three.

C2132   **syntax error : unexpected identifier**

The QuickC compiler encountered an identifier unexpectedly, resulting in a syntax error.

C2133   '*identifier*' **: unknown size**

A declaration tried to declare an array as a local variable without specifying the array's size.

C2134   *identifier* **: struct/union too large**

QuickC supports only those unions and structures whose size is less than the compiler limit of 2^{32} bytes.

C2137   **empty character constant**

C does not support an empty-character constant (''). To specify a null character, use the escape sequence '\0'.

C2138   **unmatched close comment '*/'**

The QuickC compiler detected a closing comment delimiter (*/) that didn't have a matching opening comment delimiter (/*). This error usually occurs when you nest commments; C does not support nested comments.

C2139   **type following '***type***' is illegal**

A declaration used an illegal type combination. See "Types" in Section 2 of this quick reference.

C2140   **argument type cannot be function returning...**

A formal parameter tried to declare a function that returns a specific type. The declaration can specify a pointer only to a function that returns a specific type.

C2141 **value out of range for enum constant**

An enumeration constant was assigned a value that is outside the range of values that type *int* supports.

C2142 **ellipsis requires three periods**

The compiler detected two periods (..) and assumed that an ellipsis (...) was intended. C uses the ellipsis to indicate a function that supports a variable number of parameters.

C2143 **syntax error : missing '***token1***' before '***token2***'**

The compiler expected to encounter '*token1*' but encountered '*token2*' instead. This error often occurs when you forget a closing parenthesis, brace, or semicolon.

C2144 **syntax error : missing '***token***' before '***type***'**

The compiler expected to encounter '*token*' but encountered '*type*' instead. This error often occurs when you forget a closing parenthesis, brace, or semicolon.

C2145 **syntax error : missing '***token***' before identifier**

The compiler expected to encounter '*token*' but encountered an identifier instead. This error often occurs when you forget the semicolon following the last variable declaration.

C2146 **syntax error : missing '***token***' before identifier '***identifier***'**

The compiler expected to encounter '*token*' but encountered the specified identifier instead. This error often occurs when you forget the semicolon following the last variable declaration.

C2147 **unknown size**

An expression tried to increment an index or a pointer to an array whose base type has not been declared, so the size of each element is unknown.

C2148 **array too large**

An array declaration exceeded the maximum legal size of 2^{32} bytes.

C2149 *identifier* **: named bit-field cannot have 0 width**

A named member within a bit field cannot have a 0-bit width. Only an unnamed bit field can have a 0-bit width.

C2150 *identifier* : **bit-field must have type int, signed int, or unsigned int**

ANSI C requires that bit fields be declared as *int*, *signed int*, or *unsigned int*.

C2151 **more than one cdecl/fortran/pascal attribute specified**

A function definition contained more than one keyword that specifies a calling convention. The *cdecl*, *fortran*, and *pascal* attributes designate how C passes arguments to a function. These attributes are mutually exclusive.

C2152 *identifier* : **pointers to functions with different attributes**

An expression tried to assign the address of a function that has one calling sequence attribute (*cdecl*, *fortran*, or *pascal*) to a pointer that is declared with another attribute.

C2153 **hex constants must have at least 1 hex digit**

The program tried to reference a hexadecimal constant by specifying only 0x or 0X. To represent a zero in hexadecimal format, use 0x0 or 0X0.

C2156 **pragma must be at outer level**

Certain pragmas must be specified outside all functions. See "Pragmas" in Section 2 of this quick reference.

C2159 **more than one storage class specified**

A declaration included more than one storage class modifier. See "Types" in Section 2 of this quick reference.

C2160 **## cannot occur at the beginning of a macro definition**

The preprocessor encountered a macro definition that begins with double pound signs (##), which is illegal in C. The double pound signs are used within a macro definition to concatenate the arguments on either side of them.

C2161 **## cannot occur at the end of a macro definition**

The preprocessor encountered a macro definition that ends with double pound signs (##), which is illegal in C. The double pound signs are used within a macro definition to concatenate the arguments on either side of them.

C2162   **expected macro formal parameter**

The token that followed a stringizing operator (#) in a macro definition was not one of the macro's formal parameters. The stringizing operator makes the value of the parameter that follows it a string.

C2165   '*keyword*' : **cannot modify pointers to data**

A declaration tried to use a *cdecl*, *fortran*, or *pascal* keyword to modify a pointer to data. These keywords are valid only before function names.

C2166   **lval specifies 'const' object**

An expression tried to modify the value of a variable that is declared with the *const* storage class specifier.

C2171   '*operator*' : **bad operand**

An expression tried to use a unary operator with an invalid data type.

C2172   *function* : **actual is not a pointer : parameter** *number*

A function call tried to pass a nonpointer argument to a function that expects a pointer for that parameter number.

C2173   *function* : **actual is not a pointer : parameter** *number*, **parameter list** *number*

A function call tried to pass a nonpointer argument to a function that expects a pointer for that parameter number. The first *number* indicates the parameter number in question. The second *number* indicates the argument list that contained the invalid argument.

C2174   *function* : **actual has type 'void' : parameter** *number*, **parameter list** *number*

A function call tried to pass a void argument to a function that expects a pointer for that parameter number. The first *number* indicates the parameter number in question. The second *number* indicates the argument list that contained the invalid argument.

C2175   *function* : **unresolved external**

The specified function was not found in the source file or in the default QuickC library. Either define the function in a source file or, if possible, link with a library that contains the function.

C2176   **static huge data not supported**

The QuickC environment does not let you declare a variable as *static huge*. Instead, use a pointer to the variable.

C2177   **constant too big**

The value of the specified constant was too large to assign to the specified variable.

C2180   **controlling expression has type 'void'**

The controlling expression in an *if*, *while*, *for*, or *do* statement is a function that returns type *void*. Functions of type *void* do not return a value.

C2181   **pragma requires command line option '*option*'**

The check_pointer pragma requires that you either use the /Zr compiler option from the command line or choose the Pointer Check option in the QuickC environment.

C2182   *'identifier'* **: has type 'void'**

A declaration attempted to create a variable of type *void*. Type *void* is valid only in function declarations. Variables can be pointers only to type *void (void *)*.

C2187   **cast of near function pointer to far function pointer**

C does not let you cast a near function pointer to a far function pointer.

C2188   **#error** : *message*

The program contained the #error preprocessor directive, resulting in the error message displayed. See "Preprocessor directives" in Section 2 of this quick reference.

C2201   *'function'* **: storage class must be extern**

This error occurs when you compile with the /Za option and a function is declared within a block but without the *extern* keyword.

C2202   **'interrupt' function must be 'far'**

A function to be used as an interrupt handler must be declared with the *far* keyword.

C2203 *'identifier'* **function cannot be 'pascal/fortran'**

The specified function cannot be compiled with the *pascal* or *fortran* calling sequence attributes. Functions that support a variable number of parameters or that interrupt processing cannot be declared with these keywords.

C2204 **'saveregs/interrupt' modifiers mutually exclusive**

A function can be declared as *saveregs* or *interrupt*, but it cannot be declared as both.

C2205 *'identifier'* **: cannot initialize 'extern' block scoped variables**

In a function, C does not allow the initialization of *extern* variables whose scope is that of a block.

C2206 *'function-name'* **: typedefs cannot be used for function definition**

C does not allow a user-defined type that was created with a *typedef* statement to define a function.

NOTE: The following error messages relate to QuickC's in-line assembly-language capabilities.

C2400 **inline syntax error** *'context'*, **found** *'token'*

The compiler encountered the specified token, resulting in a syntax error.

C2401 *'identifier'* **: register must be base** *'context'*

In this case, the register used with an indirect memory operand must be a base register.

C2402 *'identifier'* **: register must be index** *'context'*

In this case, the register used with an indirect memory operand must be an index register.

C2403 *'identifier'* **: register must be base/index** *'context'*

In this case, the register used with an indirect memory operand must be either a base or an index register.

C2404 *'identifier'* **: illegal register** *'context'*

The register used in this context is invalid.

C2405 **Illegal short forward reference with offset**

A short forward reference can refer only to a label.

C2406 *'identifier'* **: name undefined** *'context'*

An identifier used with a SIZE or a LENGTH operator or as a specifier with a member-selection operator (.) is not defined.

C2407 **illegal float register** *'context'*

The specified statement used an NDP register illegally.

C2408 **illegal type on PTR operator** *'context'*

The first argument used for a PTR operator was an invalid type.

C2409 **illegal type used as operator** *'context'*

The statement tried to use a type as an operator.

C2410 *'identifier'* **: ambiguous member name** *'context'*

The specified identifier was a member name for more than one structure or union. If possible, reference the member by using the name of the structure or union and the name of the member.

C2411 *'identifier'* **: illegal struct/union member** *'context'*

The specified identifier was not a member of a structure or a union or was not a member of the structure or the union specified with the member-selection operator (.).

C2412 *'identifier'* **: label redefined**

The specified label occurred more than one time in the current function. A label specifies a location in your function, and each label name must be unique.

C2413 *'token'* **: illegal align size**

The size argument in the ALIGN directive was either not specified or invalid.

C2414 **illegal number of operands**

The specified statement included an invalid number of operands. Verify that you have separated the operands with commas correctly.

C2415 **improper operand type**

One or more of the specified operands was invalid for this opcode.

C2416 *'identifier'* **: illegal opcode for processor**

The specified opcode was invalid for the current processor. Some instructions are specific to one processor, so you will receive an error message when you use them with the wrong processor.

C2417 **divide by zero** *'context'*

The denominator in a division operation was 0.

C2418 *'identifier'* **: not in a register**

An in-line assembly instruction tried to reference a variable that was declared with the *register* storage class, but the variable had not been allocated in a register. Remove the *register* keyword from the variable's definition and recompile.

C2419 **mod by zero** *'context'*

The second operand in a modulus operation was 0.

C2420 *'identifier'* **: illegal symbol** *'context'*

The specified identifier was invalid in this context.

C2421 **PTR operator used with register** *name*

The PTR operator cannot be used with a register operand.

C2422 **illegal segment override** *'context'*

The segment override in this context was invalid.

C2424 *'token'* **: improper expression** *'context'*

The use of the specified token formed an improper expression.

C2425 *'token'* **: non-constant expression** *'context'*

The use of the specified token formed a nonconstant expression in this context.

C2426 *'token'* **: illegal operator** *'context'*

The specified token cannot be used as an operator in this context.

C2427 *'identifier'* **: jump referencing label is out of range**

The program could not jump to the specified label because it was too far away. If possible, reduce the size of the main program by creating functions and calling them from within the program.

C2429 *<label>* : **illegal far label reference**

In-line assembly code specified a far call or far jump to a label, which is illegal. Far calls or far jumps should never be necessary because the scope of a label covers only a function, and a function cannot be larger than a segment.

Warning messages

The following are compiler warning messages that alert you to potential problems but do not interfere with compiling and linking.

C4000 **UNKNOWN WARNING**
Contact Microsoft Technical Support

The compiler encountered an unknown error condition. If you cannot determine what caused the warning, call Microsoft's Product Support Services group at (206) 454-2030.

C4002 **too many actual parameters for macro '***identifier***'**

The program referenced the specified macro with more parameters than were declared in the macro's formal parameter list.

C4003 **not enough actual parameters for macro '***identifier***'**

The program referenced the specified macro with fewer parameters than were declared in the macro's formal parameter list.

C4004 **missing close parenthesis after 'defined'**

An #if defined preprocessor directive was missing a closing parenthesis.

C4005 **'***identifier***' : redefinition**

The specified identifier has been defined already. This error sometimes occurs when a function definition does not match a previous function declaration.

C4006 **#undef expected an identifier**

The preprocessor encountered an #undef preprocessor directive that did not specify the name of the macro or constant to be undefined. See "Preprocessor directives" in Section 2 of this quick reference.

C4009   **string too big, trailing characters truncated**

A character string exceeded the compiler's limit.

C4011   **identifier truncated to '***identifier***'**

QuickC supports only identifiers up to 31 characters in length and truncates identifiers that are over 31 characters.

C4012   **float constant in a cross compilation**

The compiler encountered a floating-point constant in a source file being compiled for a different processor. The error message is a warning that the other processor might store floating-point values differently from the way the processor you're using stores those values.

C4014   **'***identifier***' : bit-field type must be unsigned**

A bit field must be declared as *unsigned*. In this case, the compiler converted the bit field to type *unsigned* as required.

C4015   **'***identifier***' : bit-field type must be integral**

A bit field must be declared as *unsigned*. In this case, the compiler converted the bit field to type *unsigned* as required.

C4016   **'***identifier***' : no function return type, using 'int' as default**

The specified function was neither defined nor declared. As a result, the compiler by default uses *int* as the type that the function returns. If the default is not correct, declare the function within your program.

C4017   **cast of int expression to far pointer**

A far pointer is a 32-bit value. A cast of an integer value to a far pointer might result in a meaningless value.

C4020   **'***identifier***' : too many actual parameters**

The program called a function with more parameters than were defined in the argument-type list or in the function definition.

C4021   **'***identifier***' : too few actual parameters**

The program called a function with fewer parameters than were defined in the argument-type list or in the function definition.

C4022 *'identifier'* : **pointer mismatch : parameter** *n*

The pointer type that was specified in the actual parameter list differed from the pointer type specified in the argument-type list or in the function definition.

C4024 *'identifier'* : **different types : parameter** *n*

The parameter type that was specified as an actual parameter differed from the type specified in the argument-type list or in the function definition.

C4026 **function was declared with formal argument list**

A function's argument-type list stated that a function supported parameters. The function's definition, however, did not include formal parameters.

C4027 **function was declared without formal argument list**

A function's argument-type list stated that the function did not support parameters (*void* keyword was in the argument-type list). The actual function definition, however, included formal parameters.

C4028 **parameter** *n* **declaration different**

The type of an actual parameter that was passed to a function was not the same as the parameter type that was defined in the function's argument-type list.

C4029 **declared parameter list different from definition**

A function's argument-type list did not agree with the function's declaration of formal parameters in the function definition.

C4030 **first parameter list is longer than the second**

The program declared the function twice. Each declaration specified a different parameter list for the function.

C4031 **second parameter list is longer than the first**

The program declared the function twice. Each declaration specified a different parameter list for the function.

C4032 **unnamed struct/union as parameter**

The type of a union or a structure that was passed as a parameter was unnamed. The declaration of the formal parameter must specify the type.

C4033 **function must return a value**

Unless you specifically declare a function as *void*, the function must return a value.

C4034 **sizeof returns 0**

The operand used in conjunction with the *sizeof* operator returned a length of zero bytes.

C4035 *identifier* : **no return value**

Unless you specifically declare a function as *void*, the function must return a value.

C4036 **unexpected formal parameter list**

The compiler encountered and ignored an unexpected formal parameter list in a function declaration.

C4037 **'***identifier***' : formal parameters ignored**

The list of formal parameters for a function did not include parameter types. The compiler ignored the parameters.

C4038 **'***identifier***' : formal parameter has bad storage class**

For formal parameters, C supports only the *register* and *auto* storage-class modifiers.

C4039 **'***identifier***' : function used as an argument**

A formal parameter to a function cannot be a function. Instead, the parameter should be declared as a pointer to a function.

C4040 **near/far/huge on '***identifier***' ignored**

The *near*, *far*, or *huge* keyword does not affect the specified identifier. The compiler ignored the keyword.

C4041 **formal parameter '***identifier***' is redefined**

The function declared a local variable that uses the same name as the specified formal parameter. As a result, the function was unable to reference the actual parameter.

C4042 **'***identifier***' : has bad storage class**

QuickC could not use the storage-class modifier in this case. Instead, QuickC will use the default storage class.

C4044   **huge on '*identifier*' ignored, must be an array**

QuickC allows the *huge* keyword to be used only in array declarations.

C4045   **'*identifier*' : array bounds overflow**

The number of initial values in an array declaration exceeded the number of array elements. The compiler ignored the extra initializers.

C4046   **'&' on function/array, ignored**

The program tried to use the address operator (&) on a function or an array. C lets you use the address operator on specific array elements, but using the address operator on an array name is redundant.

C4047   **'*operator*' : different levels of indirection**

An expression using the specified operator used pointers that had different levels of indirection.

C4048   **array's declared subscripts different**

The program declared the same array more than one time and with different sizes. The compiler used the largest array size that was specified.

C4049   **'*operator*' : indirection to different types**

An expression used the indirection operator (∗) to access a value of a different type.

C4051   **data conversion**

Two data values in an expression had different types. To evaluate the expression, the compiler had to convert the type of one of the values. As a result, data might have been truncated.

C4053   **at least one void operand**

An expression referenced another expression of type *void*. This error occurs when an expression uses the result of a function that returns type *void*.

C4058   **address of frame variable taken, DS != SS**

The program's data segment and stack segment were not equal. The program tried to access a frame variable by using a near pointer.

C4060 **conversion of long address to short address**

A long address is a 32-bit segment/offset address. A short address is a 16-bit offset address. The conversion of a long address to a short address resulted in the loss of the segment address.

C4061 **long/short mismatch in argument: conversion supplied**

The base types of an actual and a formal parameter differed. The compiler converted the actual parameter's type to match that of the formal parameter.

C4062 **near/far mismatch in argument: conversion supplied**

The pointer types of an actual and a formal parameter differed. The compiler converted the actual parameter's type to match that of the formal parameter.

C4067 **unexpected characters following '*directive*' directive - newline expected**

The preprocessor encountered additional characters following a preprocessor directive such as #endif. The preprocessor ignored the additional characters.

C4068 **unknown pragma**

The specified pragma was unknown to QuickC. A pragma is a preprocessor directive; QuickC supports four different pragmas. See "Pragmas" in Section 2 of this quick reference.

C4069 **conversion of near pointer to long integer**

The compiler converted a near pointer that contains a 16-bit address to a 32-bit long-integer value. This 32-bit value contains the near-pointer value in the least significant 16 bits and the current data segment value in the most significant 16 bits.

C4071 **'*identifier*' : no function prototype given**

The program called the specified function before the compiler encountered the function prototype.

C4074 **non standard extension used - '*extension*'**

The program uses a nonstandard Microsoft QuickC language extension. This message warns the user that portability might be a problem.

C4075 size of switch expression or case constant too large - converted to int

The expression in a *switch* statement and the switch's case constants must be integer values. In this case, the compiler truncated a value to the range of type *int*.

C4076 '*type*' : may be used on integral types only

C supports the use of the *signed* and *unsigned* type qualifiers only with integral types such as *int* or *char*.

C4077 unknown check_stack option

The format of the check_stack pragma was invalid. See "Pragmas" in Section 2 of this quick reference.

C4079 unexpected token '*token*'

The compiler encountered the specified token when it expected a different value.

C4082 expected an identifier, found '*token*'

The compiler encountered a pragma whose list of arguments was missing an identifier.

C4083 expected '(', found '*token*'

The compiler encountered a pragma in which the opening parenthesis for an argument list was missing.

C4084 expected a pragma keyword found '*token*'

The *token* following the *pragma* keyword was not an identifier. See "Pragmas" in Section 2 of this quick reference.

C4085 expected [on ¦ off]

The compiler encountered the use of an invalid option for the check_stack pragma. See "Pragmas" in Section 2 of this quick reference.

C4086 expected [1 ¦ 2 ¦ 4]

The compiler encountered an invalid option for the pack pragma. See "Pragmas" in Section 2 of this quick reference.

C4087 '*name*' : declared with 'void' parameter list

The program called a function that passed actual parameters when the function was declared with a *void* parameter list.

C4088   '*name*' : **pointer mismatch : parameter** *n*, **parameter list** *number*

A pointer argument to the specified function had a different level of indirection than the corresponding formal parameter.

C4089   '*name*' : **different types : parameter** *n*, **parameter list** *number*

The type of an actual parameter to a function differed from the type of a corresponding formal parameter.

C4090   **different '***const***' attributes**

A pointer to a variable of type *const* was passed to a function whose corresponding argument was a pointer to a variable that was not of type *const*.

C4091   **no symbols were declared**

The compiler encountered a declaration that specified only a type and not an identifier.

C4092   **untagged enum/struct/union declared no symbols**

The compiler encountered a declaration of an untagged structure that did not specify any members.

C4093   **unescaped newline in character constant in non-active code**

A newline ('\n') character appeared in a character constant in inactive code. Inactive code is code that is present in the source file but is not included during compilation because it follows an #if, #ifdef, or #ifndef preprocessor directive whose expression evaluated to false.

C4095   **expected ')', found '***token***'**

The compiler encountered more than one argument in a pragma that requires only one argument.

C4098   **void function returning a value**

A function declared as void tried to return a value by using the *return* statement.

C4100   '*name*' : **unreferenced formal parameter**

A formal parameter was declared but was never used in the function's code.

C4101   **'*name*' : unreferenced local variable**

A local variable was declared but was never used in the function's code.

C4102   **'*name*' : unreferenced label**

A label was declared, but it was never used in the function's code.

C4103   **'*name*' : function definition used as prototype**

The compiler encountered the function definition before the function prototype. As a result, the compiler will use the definition as the prototype throughout the program.

C4105   *name* **: code modifiers only on function or pointer to function**

The program tried to use the *cdecl*, *fortran*, or *pascal* code modifier on an identifier other than a function or a pointer to a function.

C4109   **unexpected identifier '*token*'**

The line contained an unexpected identifier. The compiler ignored the identifier.

C4110   **unexpected token 'int constant'**

The line contained an unexpected integer constant. The compiler ignored the integer constant.

C4111   **unexpected token 'string'**

The line contained an unexpected string. The compiler ignored the string.

C4112   **macro name '*string*' is reserved,** *command* **ignored**

A #define preprocessor directive tried to redefine a predefined macro or a predefined constant. The compiler ignored the directive.

C4113   **function parameter lists differed**

A statement assigned a function pointer to another function pointer. The pointer types, however, refer to functions that have different parameter lists.

C4114 **same type qualifier used more than once**

A declaration tried to use the same type qualifier (*const*, *volatile*, *signed*, or *unsigned*) more than one time in the same type. See "Types" in Section 2 of this quick reference.

C4115 **'*tag*' : type definition in formal parameter list**

A formal parameter list defined a *union*, a *struct*, or an *enum* type that specifies a tag.

C4116 **'<no tag>' : type definition in formal parameter list**

A formal parameter list defined a *union*, a *struct*, or an *enum* type that does not specify a tag.

C4118 **pragma not supported**

QuickC does not support the specified pragma. See "Pragmas" in Section 2 of this quick reference.

NOTE: The following warnings relate to QuickC's in-line assembly-language capabilities.

C4401 **'*identifier*' : member is bitfield**

The specified identifier is a bit field.

C4402 **must use PTR operator**

The statement used a type on an operand without the PTR operator.

C4403 **illegal PTR operator**

The statement used a type and a PTR operator on an operand when PTR was invalid for the operation.

C4404 **period on directive ignored**

QuickC ignored the period that preceded the directive.

C4405 **'*identifier*' : identifier is a reserved word**

The program tried to use a reserved word as an identifier.

C4406 **operand on directive ignored**

The statement specified an operand for a directive that does not require an operand. QuickC ignored the operand.

C4407 **operand size conflict**

The sizes of two operands should match, but they do not.

C4408 '*label*' : **ambiguous label**

The specified label was defined twice with different capitalization in the C source code, and was then referenced in the in-line assembler code.

C4409 **illegal instruction size**

The instruction's form did not match the specified size.

C4410 **illegal size for operand**

One or more of the operands had an invalid size.

C4411 '*identifier*' : **symbol resolves to displacement register**

The specified identifier was a local symbol that resolved to the displacement register. As a result, the symbol can be used as an operand with another symbol.

C4412 '*identifier*' : **identifier is also assembler mnemonic**

The specified identifier is an assembly-language instruction mnemonic.

C4413 '*function*' **redefined: preceding references may be invalid**

The definition of the specified function changed between incremental compilations.

OTHER TITLES FROM MICROSOFT PRESS

MICROSOFT® QUICKC® PROGRAMMING
The Microsoft Guide to Using the QuickC Compiler

*The Waite Group: Mitchell Waite, Stephen Prata,
Bryan Costales, and Harry Henderson*

MICROSOFT QUICKC PROGRAMMING is an authoritative introduction to every significant element of Microsoft QuickC. A detailed overview of the language elements gets you started. And the scores of programming examples and tips show you how to manipulate QuickC's variable types, decision structures, functions, and pointers; how to program using the Graphics Library; how to port Pascal to QuickC; how to interface your QuickC programs with assembly language; how to use the powerful source-level debugger; and more. If you're new to C or familiar with Microsoft QuickBASIC or Pascal, MICROSOFT QUICKC PROGRAMMING is for you. If you're a seasoned programmer, you'll find solid, reliable information that's available nowhere else.

624 pages, softcover, $19.95   Order Code 86-96114

PROFICIENT C
The Microsoft Guide to Intermediate and Advanced C Programming

Augie Hansen

*"A beautifully-conceived text, clearly written and logically organized...
a superb guide."*   **Computer Book Review**

If you want to combine C with MS-DOS to produce powerful programs that run at astonishing speeds, PROFICIENT C is where you want to start. It contains a wealth of programming insights, professional know-how, and techniques to improve your programming skills. PROFICIENT C is a rich assortment of reliable, structured programming methods and techniques for designing, coding, and testing your programs. You'll discover clear, immediately useful information on the MS-DOS development environment, standard libraries and interfaces, and file- and screen-oriented programs. Here are dozens of modules and full-length utilities that you'll use again and again. Each one is practical and creative without being gimmicky. Included are programs that use sound and text-oriented visual effects and control printer modes and screen color. Other programs update file modification times, test the driver, view and print files, and display non-ASCII text.

512 pages, softcover, $22.95   Order Code 86-95710

MICROSOFT® MOUSE PROGRAMMER'S REFERENCE
Microsoft Press

Currently attached to more than one million personal computers, the Microsoft Mouse is one of the world's most popular PC peripherals and an industry standard. No software program—custom or commercial—is complete without support for the Microsoft Mouse. This guide—by a team of experts from the Hardware Division of Microsoft Corporation—enables intermediate- to advanced-level programmers to add mouse support to their programs, thus adding value and ease of use. It's both an essential reference to the mouse programming interface and a handbook for writing functional mouse menus. The two 5.25-inch companion disks include:

- MOUSE.LIB and EGA.LIB
- mouse menus
- a collection of valuable programs in BASIC, QuickBASIC, QuickC, Microsoft C, Pascal, Microsoft Macro Assembler, and FORTRAN

The MICROSOFT MOUSE PROGRAMMER'S REFERENCE is the most authoritative and value-packed reference guide on mouse programming available.

336 pages, softcover with two 5.25-inch disks, $29.95
Order Code 86-97005

ADVANCED MS-DOS® PROGRAMMING, 2nd Edition
Ray Duncan

"ADVANCED MS-DOS PROGRAMMING *is one of the most authoritative in its field…*" **PC Magazine**

ADVANCED MS-DOS PROGRAMMING has been completely revised and expanded to include MS-DOS version 4, DOS and OS/2 compatibility issues, and the new PS/2 ROM BIOS services. Ray Duncan begins his instructive guide to assembly language and C programming in the PC/MS-DOS environment with an overview of the structure and loading of MS-DOS. He addresses key programming topics, including character devices, mass storage, memory management, and process management. You will find a detailed reference section of system functions and interrupts for all current versions of MS-DOS; information on the ROM BIOS and on programming for the EGA, VGA, PC/AT, and PS/2; information on programming with version 4.0 of the Lotus/Intel/Microsoft Expanded Memory Specification; and advice on writing "well-behaved" *vs* hardware-dependent applications. The examples, ranging from programming samples to full-length utilities, are both instructive and utilitarian and were developed using the Microsoft Macro Assembler version 5.1 and the Microsoft C Compiler version 5.1.

688 pages, softcover, $24.95   Order Code 86-96668

THE MS-DOS® ENCYCLOPEDIA

Foreword by Bill Gates

"...for those with any technical involvement in the PC industry, this is the one and only volume worth reading."   **PC WEEK**

If you're a serious MS-DOS programmer, this is the ultimate reference. THE MS-DOS ENCYCLOPEDIA is an unmatched sourcebook for version-specific technical data, including annotations of more than 100 system function calls—each accompanied by C-callable, assembly language routines; for comprehensive version-specific descriptions and usage information on each of the 90 user commands—the most comprehensive ever assembled; and for documentation of a host of key programming utilities. Articles cover debugging, TSRs, installable device drivers, writing applications for upward compatibility, and much, much more. THE MS-DOS ENCYCLOPEDIA contains hundreds of hands-on examples and thousands of lines of code, plus an index to commands and topics. Covering MS-DOS through version 3.2, with a special section on version 3.3, this encyclopedia is the preeminent, most authoritative reference for every professional MS-DOS programmer.

1600 pages, 7¾ x 10, hardcover, $134.95   Order Code 86-96122
            softcover, $69.95   Order Code 86-96833

ADVANCED OS/2 PROGRAMMING

Ray Duncan

Here is the most complete and accurate source of information on the new features and structure of OS/2 for C and assembly language programmers. Topics include porting existing MS-DOS applications to OS/2, programming in both real and protected modes, writing true multitasking programs, and more. ADVANCED OS/2 PROGRAMMING contains an example-packed reference section on the more than 250 OS/2 1.1 kernel functions, with complete information on their calling arguments, return values, and special uses. ADVANCED OS/2 PROGRAMMING will improve your capability as an OS/2 programmer.

800 pages, softcover, $24.95   Order Code 86-96106

INSIDE OS/2

Gordon Letwin, Chief Architect, Systems Software, Microsoft
Foreword by Bill Gates

"Mere recommendations aren't good enough for INSIDE OS/2.... If you're at all serious about OS/2 you must buy this book."

Dr. Dobb's Journal

INSIDE OS/2 is an unprecedented, candid, and exciting technical examination of OS/2. Letwin takes you inside the philosophy, key development issues, programming implications, and future of OS/2. He also provides the first in-depth look at each of OS/2's design elements—how it works alone and its role in the system. A valuable and revealing programmer-to-programmer discussion of the graphical user interface, multitasking, memory management, protection, encapsulation, interprocess communication, direct device access, and more. You can't get a more inside view. This is a book no OS/2 programmer can afford to be without!

304 pages, softcover, $19.95   Order Code 86-96288

THE 80386 BOOK
Assembly Language Programmer's Guide for the 80386
Ross P. Nelson

If you are an experienced 8088/8086 user, this is the most comprehensive and authoritative introduction to the 80386 chip you'll find. Nelson gives you a detailed analysis of the CPU, memory architecture, the protection scheme, compatibility with 8086/80286 chips, and much more. You will gain good 80386 assembly language programming techniques through the scores of programming and design examples included in this book. A complete instruction set reference and information-packed appendixes make THE 80386 BOOK a valuable reference tool.

464 pages, softcover, $24.95   Order Code 86-96494

PROGRAMMING WINDOWS
The Microsoft® Guide to Programming for the MS-DOS® Presentation Manager: Windows 2.0 and Windows/386
Charles Petzold

PROGRAMMING WINDOWS is the first full technical discussion of Windows and your fastest route to great Windows applications. Special topics cover memory management, fonts, dynamically linkable libraries, manipulating the resources of the graphics device interface, and much more. Included are scores of valuable sample programs and utilities. Even if you have little programming experience you will gain a solid understanding of Windows' dynamics and the relationship of Windows to MS-DOS and the IBM PC.

864 pages, softcover, $24.95   Order Code 86-96049
**   hardcover, $34.95   Order Code 86-96130**

THE PROGRAMMER'S PC SOURCEBOOK
Reference Tables for IBM PCs and Compatibles, PS/2 Machines, and DOS
Thom Hogan

At last! A reference book to save you the frustration of searching high and low for key pieces of technical data. Here is important factual information culled from hundreds of sources and integrated into convenient, accessible charts, tables, and listings. It's the first place to turn for immediate, accurate information about your computer and its operating system. It's all here. THE PROGRAMMER'S PC SOURCEBOOK covers all versions of PC-DOS and MS-DOS and all IBM computers, including the PS/2 series. Tables cover DOS commands and utilities; interrupts; mouse information; EMS support; ROM BIOS calls; memory layouts; interrupt vectors; RAM parameters; keyboard-related charts; extended character set; and more.

560 pages, softcover, $24.95   Order Code 86-96296

PROGRAMMER'S GUIDE TO PC & PS/2® VIDEO SYSTEMS
Maximum Video Performance from the EGA,® VGA, HGC, and MCGA
Richard Wilton

Do you want maximum video performance from your EGA, VGA, HGC, or MCGA graphics adapter? PROGRAMMER'S GUIDE TO PC & PS/2 VIDEO SYSTEMS shows you how to achieve it. No other book offers such detailed, specialized programming data, techniques, and advice to help you tackle the exacting problems of programming directly to the video hardware. And no other book offers the more than 100 invaluable source code examples included here. Whatever graphics output you want—text, circles, region fill, bit blocks, or animation, you'll do it more quickly and more effectively with PROGRAMMER'S GUIDE TO PC & PS/2 VIDEO SYSTEMS—a one-of-a-kind resource for every serious programmer.

544 pages, softcover, $24.95   Order Code 86-96163

PROGRAMMER'S QUICK REFERENCE SERIES

STANDARD C: PROGRAMMER'S QUICK REFERENCE
P. J. Plauger & Jim Brodie

This conveniently organized, one-of-a-kind guide provides all the information you need to read and write Standard C programs that conform to the recently approved ANSI and ISO standards for the C programming language. Standard C will be used in all future standard implementations of the C language. STANDARD C: PROGRAMMER'S QUICK REFERENCE concisely describes all aspects of Standard C. Scores of diagrams illustrate the syntax rules. Whether you are new to C or familiar with an earlier dialect of C, this handy guide will be the foundation of your C programs. P. J. Plauger is the secretary of the ANSI-authorized C Programming Language Standards Committee and convenor of the ISO committee on Standard C. Jim Brodie is chairman and convenor of the ANSI-authorized C Programming Language Standards Committee.

224 pages, 4¾ x 8, softcover, $7.95   Order Code 86-96676

MS-DOS® FUNCTIONS: PROGRAMMER'S QUICK REFERENCE
Ray Duncan

This great quick reference is full of the kind of information every programmer—professional or casual—needs right at his or her fingertips. In MS-DOS FUNCTIONS, you'll find data—all clearly organized—on each MS-DOS system service call (accessed via Interrupts 20H through 2FH) along with a list of the parameters it requires, the results it returns, version dependencies, and valuable programming notes. MS-DOS FUNCTIONS covers MS-DOS through version 4.

128 pages, 4¾ x 8, softcover, $5.95   Order Code 86-96411

IBM® ROM BIOS: PROGRAMMER'S QUICK REFERENCE
Ray Duncan

If you're an assembly-language, Pascal, or C programmer—no matter what your experience level—this is an incredibly useful reference. IBM ROM BIOS: PROGRAMMER'S QUICK REFERENCE is a handy and compact guide to the ROM BIOS services of IBM PC, PC/AT, and PS/2 machines. Designed for quick and easy access to information, this guide gives you all the core information on each ROM BIOS service: its required parameters and returned results, version dependencies, and valuable programming notes. Keep this within easy reach!

128 pages, 4¾ x 8, softcover, $5.95   Order Code 86-96478

*Microsoft Press books are available
wherever fine books are sold,
or credit card orders can be placed by calling*
1-800-638-3030
(in Maryland call collect 824-7300).

Kris Jamsa

Kris Jamsa graduated from the United States Air Force Academy with a degree in computer science in 1983. Upon graduation, he moved to Las Vegas, Nevada, where he began work as a VAX/VMS system manager for the U.S. Air Force. In 1986, Jamsa received a master's degree in computer science, with an emphasis in operating systems, from the University of Nevada, Las Vegas. He then taught computer science at the National University in San Diego, California, for one year before leaving the Air Force in 1988 to begin writing full-time. He is the author of more than a dozen books on DOS, OS/2, Windows, hard-disk management, and Pascal and C programming languages. Jamsa currently resides in Las Vegas with his wife and their two daughters.

The manuscript for this book was prepared and submitted to Microsoft Press in electronic form. Text files were processed and formatted using Microsoft Word.

Cover design by Thomas A. Draper
Interior text design by Greg Hickman
Principal typography by Lisa Iversen

Text composition by Microsoft Press in Times Roman with display in Times Roman Bold, using the Magna composition system and the Linotronic 300 Laser imagesetter.